G000075236

THE WINES OF BORDEAUX

Published by
APPLE PRESS
6 Blundell Street
London N7 9BH

ISBN: 1-84092-302-4

Printed in Spain

▪ THE WINES OF ▪
BORDEAUX

GILBERT DELOS

Photographs by
Philippe Hurlin

APPLE

CONTENTS

THE WORLD OF BORDEAUX

Throughout the world, "Bordeaux" means "wine." This is not only because of the size of the winegrowing area (the largest in Europe) and the volume of wine produced each year (two percent of world production), but also and above all because the quality and diversity of its products make the Bordeaux region the standard for all wines.

This status is partly due to the region's soil and climate which are adapted to the production of wines that are considered the very best. But it is also due to an important wine trading business, which, through the port of Bordeaux, distributes the best products of the region, far beyond the domestic market to the entire world. This marriage of vines and commerce is the driving force behind the centuries-old fame of the region.

The success of Bordeaux wines can also be explained by man's amazing ability to adapt to the realities of different soils. The incredible diversity of wines produced in the Bordeaux region is the result of the close relationship between man, the soil, and the vine. Bordeaux winegrowers have ceaselessly toiled to produce wines that best express the true nature of the region.

Wine lovers will always be able to find what they are looking for in Bordeaux, from a nice little table wine to the most dazzling *grand cru,* from the driest wine to the sweetest, from the palest white to a red as dark as ink. This is a winegrowing region of incredible richness.

Left: The quays of Bordeaux. To the right, the famous Chartron quay, the headquarters of many wine merchants.
Above: The Girondins monument on the Esplanade des Quinconces in Bordeaux.

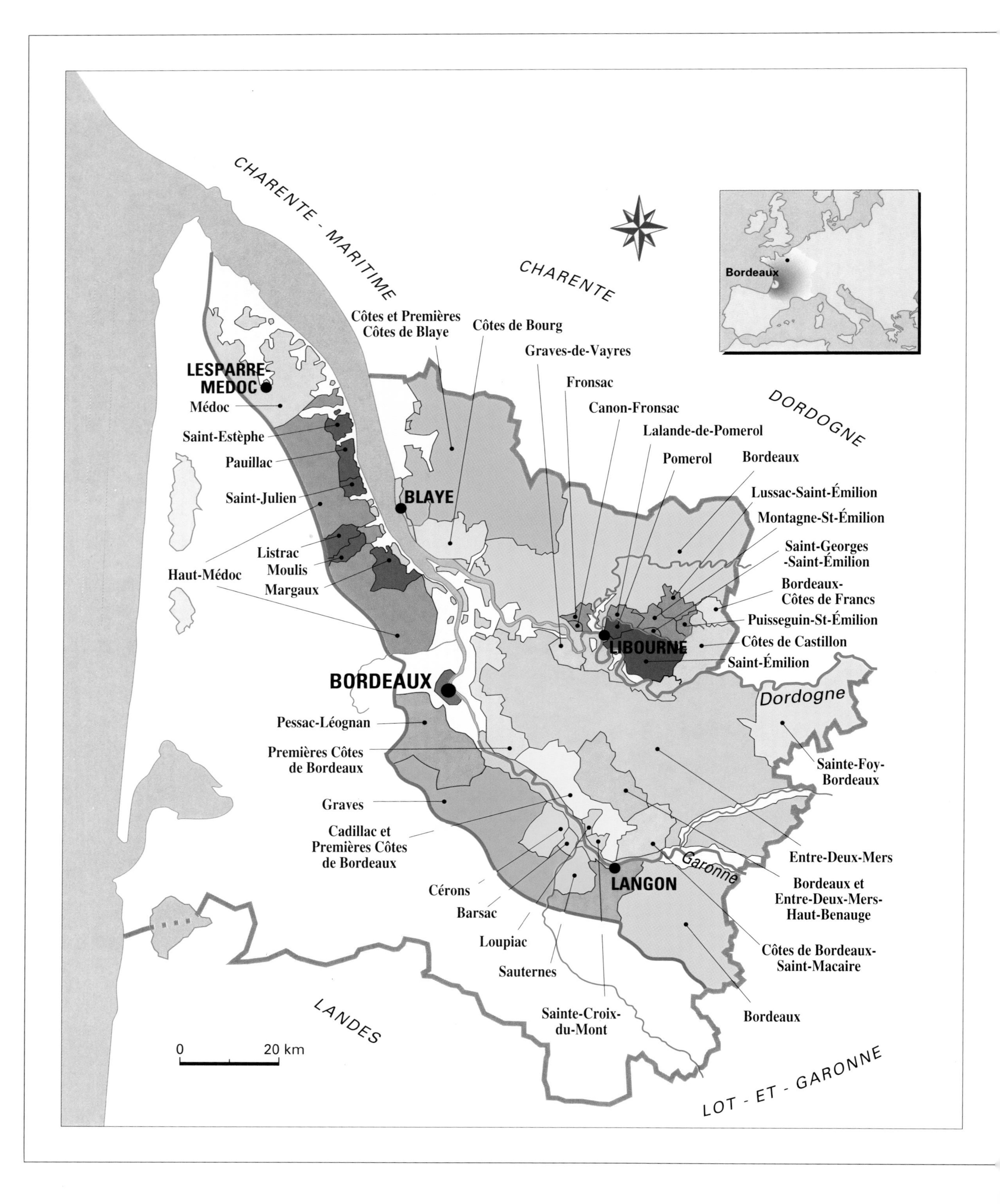
CHARENTE - MARITIME
CHARENTE
DORDOGNE
Bordeaux
Côtes et Premières
Côtes de Blaye
Côtes de Bourg
Graves-de-Vayres
Fronsac
Canon-Fronsac
Lalande-de-Pomerol
Pomerol
Bordeaux
LESPARRE-
MEDOC
Médoc
Saint-Estèphe
Pauillac
Saint-Julien
BLAYE
Lussac-Saint-Émilion
Montagne-St-Émilion
Saint-Georges
-Saint-Émilion
Listrac
Moulis
Haut-Médoc
Margaux
Bordeaux-
Côtes de Francs
Puisseguin-St-Émilion
LIBOURNE
Côtes de Castillon
Saint-Émilion
BORDEAUX
Dordogne
Pessac-Léognan
Premières Côtes
de Bordeaux
Sainte-Foy-
Bordeaux
Graves
Cadillac et
Premières Côtes
de Bordeaux
Entre-Deux-Mers
Garonne
Cérons
LANGON
Bordeaux et
Entre-Deux-Mers-
Haut-Benauge
Barsac
Loupiac
Côtes de Bordeaux-
Saint-Macaire
Sauternes
LANDES
Sainte-Croix-
du-Mont
Bordeaux
0
20 km
LOT - ET - GARONNE

A GEOGRAPHY INFLUENCED BY HISTORY

With more than 271,700 acres of *appellations d'origine contrôlée,* the Bordeaux wine region alone is equal in size to the entire national winegrowing areas of Germany, South Africa, and Hungary, and twice the size of those in Australia. In France, Bordeaux's vineyards equal the combined vineyards of the Côtes du Rhône, Alsace, and the Loire Valley. While the vineyards of Languedoc-Roussillon are much larger (864,500 acres), they produce mostly lesser wines without controlled appellations.

Vineyards take up most of the Gironde department (the largest of France's ninety-five administrative divisions), except in areas unsuited to winegrowing, mostly located near the Atlantic coast. The department is divided into three regions bordered principally by two rivers, the Garonne and the Dordogne, and the Gironde estuary.

- Graves, on the left banks of the Garonne and Gironde, includes, from north to south, all the Médoc appellations (with six commune *appellations d'origine contrôlée*), as well as those of Graves and the sweet wines (Cérons, Barsac, and Sauternes).
- Entre-deux-Mers, between the Dordogne and the Garonne Rivers, groups together the following appellations: Entre-deux-Mers, Premières Côtes de Bordeaux, Cadillac, Loupiac, Sainte-Croix-du-Mont, Sainte-Foy-Bordeaux, Graves de Vayres, Côtes de Bordeaux-Saint-Macaire. This region also produces large volumes of Bordeaux and Bordeaux Supérieurs.
- Libourne and Blaye-Bourg, on the right bank of the Dordogne River, produces the following appellations: Fronsac, Canon-Fronsac, Pomerol, Lalande de Pomerol, Saint-Émilion and its four adjuncts (Lussac, Montagne, Puisseguin, and Saint-Georges), Côtes de Castillon, and Côtes-de-Francs. On the right bank of the Gironde are the Blaye, Premières Côtes de Blaye, and Côtes de Bourg appellations.

The development of these vineyards was anything but linear. Their history has been marked by a number of upheavals over the centuries. Some vineyards have disappeared and been replanted over and over again, while others, like those of the Médoc, are relatively recent because the area for a long time had an inhospitable climate, while vines prospered in Graves and Libourne.

The special soil of the Graves vineyards is made up of a mixture of gravel and sand.

Landscape, Soil, and Climate

The Bordeaux region is not uniformly covered with vineyards. In the Médoc and Libourne, there are vines almost everywhere, and a château planted in the middle of a vast plot of vines is a common sight.

The "château" might be a lordly residence surrounded by parks and gardens, a large house (sometimes called a "chartreuse"), or even a simple farmhouse set up for winemaking. In the Gironde, "château" is simply a legal term designating a particular viticultural estate (even if there are no residential buildings on it) and the wines it produces.

Right: a Médoc vineyard. The drainage qualities of the soil contribute to the exceptional wines from some areas of this region.

Entre-deux-Mers also has huge viticultural estates, but the landscape is less consistent, with large areas cultivated in other products or covered with forests.

The vineyards of Graves, which used to be more extensive, were gradually broken up by attacks of powdery mildew and phylloxera in the nineteenth century, allowing the forest to invade. Creeping urbanization has also aggravated the problem, causing some vineyards, such as Haut-Brion, to find themselves located practically in the heart of towns.

Although the ground in the Aquitaine region is basically made up of limestone, the deposits left by glaciers, rivers, and the wind have created soils of great diversity.

While a soil's makeup has an important influence on the quality of the wine ultimately produced, it must not be forgotten that wines of widely varying quality can sometimes issue from grapes grown in similar soils, particularly those with a high gravel content.

The most important factor is drainage; in other words, the ability of the soil to eliminate or retain water is largely responsible for differences in quality from one plot of land to another. While a vine must "suffer" to produce a great wine, meaning that the roots have to go relatively deep in search of the water it needs, it nevertheless has to have a certain quantity of water during the crucial stages of its growth.

The vineyards of the Saint-Émilion district stretch across low hills overlooking the Dordogne River.

In the Gironde, there are four main types of soil:

• A mixture of sand and gravel, called *graves*, with variable proportions of clay and silt. Its drainage capacity enables it to produce some of the greatest Bordeaux wines.

In the Médoc and Graves, this type of soil forms a continuous band ranging from 1.9 miles to 9.3 miles in width, and with a depth that varies from a few feet to several yards. It is also found in Libourne, Pomerol, and in parts of Saint-Émilion, as well as in the small area of Graves de Vayres, on the left bank of the Dordogne River.

• Clay-limestone soil, composed of a base of limestone with a more or less thick layer of clay on top of it, found primarily in Libourne and Sauternes. Drainage capacity depends on how deep the limestone layer is buried.

• *Molasse,* or sandstone, formed by silt deposited by the wind, found primarily in the center of Entre-deux-Mers.

• Alluvial soil, formed more recently on the banks of the rivers, called *palus* in the region. It is very rich but often has poor drainage capacities.

Finally, there is an odd type of soil in a few viticultural sites in the Gironde; it is made up of oyster shell and other seashell deposits dating to the Quaternary era (the most recent period in earth's history, stretching over a span of nearly two million years). This type of soil can be found in Sainte-Croix-du-Mont, where it has become something of a tourist attraction.

Bordeaux's climate is basically warm and humid, and is consistent over the whole region since the absence of natural barriers allows the Atlantic to exert its influence over the whole area. The winters are fairly warm, allowing the vines to begin their vegetative cycle early. There are, however, real risks of springtime freezes, which can have disastrous effects on developing vine stock.

Rainfall is the other factor that causes variations in vintages. The total volume of precipitation is fairly constant from one year to another (between 31 and 35 inches on average), with dry years (less than 21.5 inches of rain) such as 1921, 1948, and 1953 being the exception.

The quality of a harvest depends primarily on the weather during the final weeks of summer and the first days of autumn, and great years are generally marked by sunny days during those periods. Nevertheless, thanks to their wine-making expertise, most growers know how to make the best of the most difficult conditions, and they, rather than the weather, are increasingly responsible for the final quality of the wine. For example, 1991, a year marked by rain and frost, even saw some good results.

Vineyards share the land with other crops and forests in the Entre-deux-Mers region.

MAKING AND SELLING WINE

It goes without saying that nature played a major role in the establishment and development of the Bordeaux vineyards, but other factors have also made a difference, including man's skill in winemaking and aptitude for selling the product. The people of the Gironde have shown themselves to have a successful combination of these two qualities.

A Bordeaux saying has it that wine was known before the vine. In the first century, Campanian merchants were already doing business in the region, which had been recently colonized by the Romans. The Romans were in all likelihood responsible for the planting of the first vines, as they were in other parts of Gaul. Ausonius, the Latin poet born in Bordeaux, was famous for his vineyards, whose vestiges are still being sought in Saint-Émilion.

As in the rest of the ancient world, the wine produced in the Gironde was exclusively consumed locally for many years, and the vines suffered regularly from damage caused by the Vikings and other invaders.

Symbolically speaking, May 18, 1152, marks the true birth of the Bordeaux vineyards. On that day, Eleanor of Aquitaine married Henry Plantagenet, the future king of England. Her dowry included a large part of the west of France, including Guyenne. The Bordeaux region did not become French territory again until 1453, after the battle of Castillon.

During those three centuries, the wines of Bordeaux became known to and loved by English and other northern European consumers. Because Aquitaine and England belonged to the same political entity, administrative matters were simplified, and thanks to the Gironde estuary that provided easy access to the sea, trading companies were successful in selling the region's products abroad. They also benefited from a veritable monopoly on the northern European wine market, to the detriment of other French regions that lacked access to it.

A glass bung is placed upon barrels to identify first-year wines.

However, the overall goal was to market all the wines of Bordeaux, not only those of Aquitaine. The Graves and Libourne vineyards did, in fact, furnish the clarets that the Anglo-Saxons were so fond of, but the merchants also sold wines from throughout southwestern of France, depending on the results of the harvests.

Beginning in the eighteenth century, the situation changed considerably because of the rising reputation of Médoc. Long neglected, this region benefited from the wealth that the middle class of Bordeaux accumulated over several centuries of intense commercial activity. The wines proved to be of great quality, and the British were quickly hooked on the "new French claret." It was, in fact, London merchants who undertook the barrel-aging of the wine, which they bought as soon as the fermentation was completed.

The place of origin of a wine gradually became associated with its quality, and the Bordeaux merchants eventually began to bottle the wine in their own establishments. Until the end of the nineteenth century, most of Bordeaux's wines left the famous quais des Chartrons in the port of Bordeaux in barrels. During the long voyage, the wines acquired a distinctive aroma known as their *goût bordeaux,* or "Bordeaux taste," a term that persists to this day.

At the turn of the nineteenth century, a hierarchy of the different Bordeaux growing areas was established. The names of the best vineyards were already known to the most enlightened wine experts, who definitively classified them in 1855. The century, however, would not be a good one for winegrowing.

British market were closed to French producers during most of the years of Napoleon's regime. Then, powdery mildew (beginning in 1851), downy mildew, and especially phylloxera ravaged the crops, necessitating the complete replanting of the vineyards.

Once again, the merchants played an important role, this time in the choice of new types of vines (such as the sémillon used in Entre-deux-Mers) and in the dissemination of the new oenological discoveries of Pasteur and his students. While the merchants couldn't do much about the quality of the wines while the vines were growing, they could at least correct the most blatant faults when bottling them.

Origin and Quality

The end of the nineteenth and the beginning of the twentieth century saw the establishment of a system that guaranteed the quality of wines based on their origin. In 1884, the first wine producers' association was founded, in Saint-Émilion. The setting was no accident; the merchants of Libourne had been selling directly to consumers for a longer time than their neighbors, and they were aided by railroad lines linking them to the capital. They needed structures that would guarantee the provenance and therefore the quality of their products.

The decree of February 18, 1911 limited the right to a Bordeaux appellation to vineyards located in the Gironde department. This was not an easy decision; during the negotiations between winegrowers, merchants, elected officials, and bureaucrats, there had been talk of granting the right to the appellation to forty-two communities in the Dordogne and twenty-four in the Lot-et-Garonne. Three years earlier, a law had stated that an appellation should be based on "continuous local usage."

After both world wars I and world war II sales declined, vineyards were abandoned due to labor shortages, and financial crises forced owners to sell their assets precipitously. In spite of all this, the definition of an *appellation d'origine contrôlée* (AOC), which guaranteed the identity and authenticity of a vineyard, was established between the two wars by the laws of 1919, 1927, and 1935. The ideas of the "local, loyal, and continuous" use of particular vines and precise geographic limits gradually became accepted.

Aside from the wines of certain renowned vineyards and prestigious areas (Médoc or Saint-Émilion), merchants mostly sold Bordeaux wines without worrying too much about their precise origins. The laws enacted between the wars, however, brought the idea of territorial origin to the forefront, as the wine producers' associations, many of them formed in response to these laws, applied themselves to promoting the specific characteristics of the wines of their regions.

This led to the emergence of numerous appellations—previously unknown to consumers—that allowed the producers to affirm their identities. Apart from the Premières Côtes de Bordeaux or

A nineteenth-century engraving depicting the Château Haut-Brion, located in Graves at the portals of Bordeaux. Long before the importance of a wine's origins was generally acknowledged, Haut-Brion was one of the first estates to sell its wines under its own name rather than the generic denomination "Bordeaux."

THE BORDEAUX BARREL

The primary unit of measure in Bordeaux is a *tonneau,* of a capacity of 900 liters (237.8 gallons). But this is misleading, because no barrel of this size exists. It takes four *barriques,* barrels of 225 liters each (these can be seen in any Bordeaux *chai,* or wine shed) to make up the 900-liter measure.

The *tonneau* is still used to indicate the volume of wine sold in bulk, but with the growth of estate-bottling, the 75-centiliter bottle is increasingly becoming the standard measure, by the bottle or the case of 12 bottles.

Sainte-Foy-Bordeaux, they did not claim a Bordeaux origin. It was not until the 1950s that an association was formed whose purpose was to defend and to promote the wines of the entire Bordeaux region. This was the Conseil Interprofessionnel du Vin de Bordeaux, which became an officially operating organization in 1973.

In the first half of the twentieth century numerous problems led to commercial difficulties of all kinds and to the abandonment of many estates. After World War II, however, the stage was set for a new era of prosperity.

One of the major factors was the estate-bottling of wines. This inevitably led to a loss of supremacy for the merchants, while consumers around the world applauded this guarantee of origin. Knowing that the wine was produced and aged in the same place (and not in an anonymous wine shed that might be located anywhere) made them much more loyal buyers. Over time, they learned to distinguish between the different appellations, soil types, and even the vineyards and their owners.

The tendency to automatically choose a bottle of Bordeaux in a shop or restaurant is still widespread today; the majority of consumers around the world, and even in France, are still unaware of

***One of the wine cellars of the Château Ausone, an A-rated, Saint-Émilion* premier grand cru A. *Bordeaux winemakers age their wines in aboveground sheds called* chais, *while in Burgundy, wine is stored in underground cellars, or* caves. *Saint-Émilion, in fact, is the only Bordeaux region that has underground* chais.**

the differences between the various Bordeaux vineyards or their respective qualities. But this situation also proves that, thanks to the efforts of all those involved, the essential message has gotten through: the name "Bordeaux" stands for a certain level of quality.

It is revealing that nearly all of the Bordeaux region's vineyards now produce AOC wines. Table wines currently represent only two percent of total volume, even though they accounted for one-third at the beginning of the 1960s.

By the same token, white wines, which accounted for sixty percent of the region's production in 1960, now make up only fifteen percent of total volume, while overall production has more than doubled. The downturn in wine production between the two world wars and the terrible freeze of 1956 can partly explain the lesser importance of red wines at the beginning of the 1960s, but the statistics also show the marvelous ability of the Bordeaux region to adapt to changes in demand.

For many consumers who know little about wine, "Bordeaux" is a synonym for "red wine." Many people are unaware of the great diversity of the Gironde vineyards.

Professional Structures

The organization of the wine business in the Gironde might seem complicated, as it involves a large number of associations.

First, there are the winegrowers (around fifteen thousand) and the merchants (around four hundred). Each of these groups has its own associations, with thirty-six for the winegrowers and two for the merchants. These associations are organised into two separate professional federations, which, together with the wine brokers (around 150), form the Conseil Interprofessionnel du Vin de Bordeaux.

In addition to these groups others have been formed upon different criteria; these might be regional (Conseil des Vins du Médoc), cooperative, or qualitative such as the Union des Grands Crus. Finally, there are institutions like the Grand Conseil du Vin de Bordeaux, which unite the wine-tasting fraternities and the Académie du Vin de Bordeaux.

BORDEAUX: AN INTERNATIONAL STANDARD

When Thomas Jefferson, the ambassador of the newly independant confederation of former British colonies in America, was posted in France between 1784 and 1789, he devoted part of his time to wine, which was regarded as the most elegant and civilized drink of his era. Although the future president of the United States spent only four days in the Bordeaux region, he wrote passionately about the contemporary art of winegrowing in the Gironde basin.

His interest in the Bordeaux vineyards, especially in the sweet wines of Sauternes, is just one of many proofs of the longstanding reputation of the wines of Bordeaux (True, he misspelled the name of the great Château d'Yquem as "Diquem," but does this really matter?). Even in Jefferson's time, the wines of Médoc and Graves were considered to be the best. We even have a souvenir of Jefferson's visit: a 1784 bottle of Château d'Yquem engraved with his initials.

In the Middle Ages, with a steadfastness that could not be deterred by political instability, Bordeaux's traders built a reputation for the region's wines abroad: first in Great Britain, then in northern Europe, and finally in the rest of the world.

Today, one-third of the volume of wine produced in Bordeaux (47.5 million gallons in the 1993-94 season) is exported. Three-quarters of these exports are absorbed within the European Union. The United States imports nearly seven percent (ten percent in value), with a marked preference for the *grands crus.*

The greatest advantage of the Bordeaux region is certainly the wide range of wines that it can produce: the breeding and distinction of the Médocs, the vigor and depth of the Saint-Émilions and Pomerols, the harmony and unity of the red and white

Graves, the sumptuous blossoming of the sweet wines of Sauternes. But we must not forget all the other Bordeaux that simply provide the assurance of well-made, agreeable wines.

Beyond commercial considerations, the wines of Bordeaux represent an unshakeable standard for all other wine producers. The best wines from around the world are always judged against the wines of Bordeaux. And while it occasionally happens during a competitive tasting that an Italian or American wine takes first place in the rankings, it is always in the company of the wines of the Gironde.

When a recent medical study showed that moderate consumption of red wine is good for one's health, especially in preventing cardiovascular problems, the press immediately dubbed the phenomenon the "French paradox," provoking an increase in the consumption of Bordeaux in the United States.

Today, American tasters and experts dominate the wine market. Like Robert Parker, the best known among them, they determine the sales of the Bordeaux crus and vintages by ranking them on a scale of 100. This has so become the rule that in 1996, at the initiative of the Savour Club, a European Grand Jury was formed to counterbalance the supremacy of the Americans. Its first tasting brought together twenty-one wine professionals from all over Europe to judge twenty-two Bordeaux *grands crus,* plus a single fine Italian wine to serve as a trap!

And, whenever there is a dispute between the Old and New World schools of thought, it is always the wines of Bordeaux that are at the center of the debate.

Opposite page: A bottle of Château d'Yquem 1784 that belonged to Thomas Jefferson, whose initials are engraved on it. This is probably one of the oldest bottles known today.

Preparations for a tasting of different vintages in the kitchen of the Château Prieuré-Lichine in Médoc. This estate was bought in 1951 by Alexis Lichine, author of the famous **Encyclopedia of Wines and Spirits.** *In his works, Lichine tried to impart a better understanding of Bordeaux to readers throughout the world. The estate is now managed by his son, Sacha.*

THE ADVANTAGES OF QUALITY

In addition to the soil and the climate, the wines of Bordeaux depend on other important factors: the care of the vine, and growing and winemaking techniques. Throughout their entire history, the winemakers of Bordeaux have never stopped reassessing, questioning, and perfecting their methods, and seeking new ways of improving the quality of their wines.

Specific Vines

The Bordeaux region has always produced both red and white wines, but the proportions have varied according to the time period and to the fashions in wine consumption.

In Bordeaux, three dominant grape varieties are used in the making of red wines. These vines all descend from cuttings and the selective breeding of an older variety, *Vitis biturica,* which is named after an ancient Gallic tribe that once lived in Aquitaine. The existence of these three varieties and their mixture in variable proportions are the keys to winemaking in the Bordeaux region. In some regions such as Burgundy only a single grape variety is used in the making of wines. In other regions, the Côtes-du-Rhône for example, several different grape varieties are used.

The cabernet sauvignon, even though it is harvested late and sometimes has difficulty maturing, is perfectly adapted to the conditions of Bordeaux since the soil in which it grows best is a mixture of sand and gravel. The cabernet sauvignon makes a well-constituted wine with strong earthy aromas. It accounts for the majority of vines in Médoc, but is much rarer elsewhere, especially in Libourne.

The cabernet franc, in spite of its similar name, is quite different from the cabernet sauvignon. More vigorous, it yields less-structured wines that are best. That but have more aromatic finesse. In Saint-Émilion, it is often called *bouchet* or *bouchet blanc,* and, in Médoc, it is sometimes known as *grand carmenet* or *gros cabernet.*

The merlot, which appeared in the eighteenth century, is not unlike cabernet franc. Merlot is so named because blackbirds (*merles,* in French) like to eat the the grape, or perhaps because its color is similar to that of the bird. This fruity, early-harvest grape does not tolerate frost very well. The typical vine of Libourne, it produces a supple wine with a wide range of aromas.

Three other vines are legally authorized for the production of red wines, but they are becoming progressively rare: cot, or malbec, which is now found almost exclusively in the Côtes de Bourg area; carmenère, which has nearly disappeared; and petit-verdot, noted for its late maturity and strong acidity, which increases its capacity for aging.

For white wines, there are also three main varieties in Bordeaux. One of these is sémillon, long specific to Sauternes because of its remarkable ability to form noble rot. Once winegrowers learned how to protect it from gray rot, however, it spread to other regions, lending great aromatic finesse and harmonious composition to the wines made from it.

The sauvignon (whose name refers to its *sauvage,* or wild, origins), is very common throughout French vineyards. It is vigorous but susceptible to diseases like powdery mildew. Its freshness and powerful aromas are especially noticeable in young wines.

The muscadelle is specific to the Bordeaux region and the Dordogne Valley. It produces wines that are at once acidic and well-rounded, with specific floral aromas.

Other, less-common varieties include colombard (sometimes used with sémillon) and ugni blanc, both of which are used primarily in Charente to make cognac. They have also spread into the north of the Gironde, especially Blaye. The merlot blanc is much rarer.

The Winemaking Process

Red Wines

The first step consists of fermenting the grape juice (which is obtained by crushing the grapes), along with their skin, seeds, and stems. This step gives the wine its color and tannin. This first fermentation is called the alcoholic fermentation. The goal is to transform the grape sugars into alcohol and carbon dioxide, and the process usually takes between five and ten days.

Once this fermentation is finished, the wine and skins are left to ferment together in a vat for an-

Racking at Château Lascombes in Margaux. In the 1970s, this estate was one of the first to buy ultramodern wine-making equipment.

other week. Then the wine is separated from the solid elements (the lees, or dregs) and transferred into a vat or wooden barrel; this is the *vin de goutte,* or free-run wine. The lees are pressed to extract the remaining juice, known as the *vin de presse,* or press wine.

The next step is malolactic fermentation (which sometimes takes place during the alcoholic fermentation). This stage transforms the malic acid (which has a sourish taste) into milder lactic acid and carbon dioxide. The wine can then be racked (to separate it from the remaining lees) and it is usually mixed together in the same vat with wines from different vines and different parcels of land.

This stage is important for the final quality of the wine. It is also the time when the winemaker can establish a hierarchy of wines produced on the same estate *(premier vin, deuxième vin* and so on*)* or decide to set aside the best wine to create a prestige vintage.

Once the wine has been assembled, it enters a period of rest. Aging is accomplished in vats or, more commonly, in oak barrels. The evolution of the wine is controlled by regular racking, and it is "fined" with egg whites or similar substances to draw out the minute particles suspended in it. The barrels are regularly topped off with identical wines to compensate for the loss of volume due to evaporation.

When the wine is considered satisfactory, it is bottled, either on the estate itself or in a merchant's storehouse.

White Wines

When making white wine, unlike red, careful attention is paid to avoid coloration and the extraction of tannin from the grape. As soon as the har-

Grapes with noble rot, used to make* liquoreux *white wines.

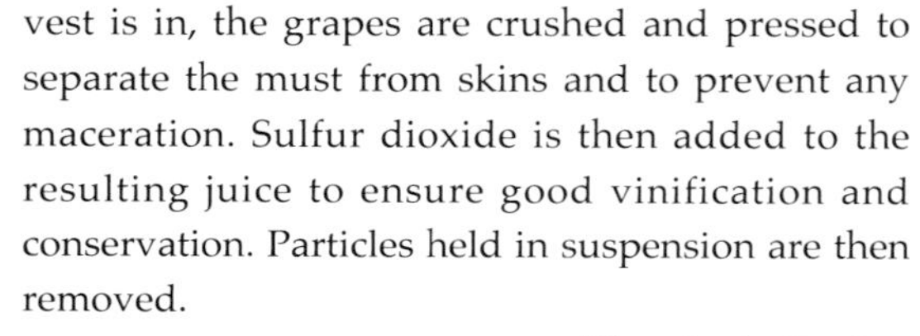

vest is in, the grapes are crushed and pressed to separate the must from skins and to prevent any maceration. Sulfur dioxide is then added to the resulting juice to ensure good vinification and conservation. Particles held in suspension are then removed.

The quality of the dry white wines of Bordeaux has improved appreciably over the past fifteen years.

The alcoholic fermentation, at a temperature of less than twenty degrees Celsius, lasts from twelve to fifteen days. The malolactic fermentation is not always done, especially if the winemaker wants a good level of acidity in his wines. For most dry white wines, the aging process is relatively short and usually accomplished in vats. The wine is bottled in the year following its harvest.

Oenological discoveries made during the past twenty years in Graves and elsewhere have made possible the making of white wines of superior quality. The new methods responsible for the improvement are primarily prolonged aging in oak barrels and aging at low temperatures. At a time when the Bordeaux region was confronted with widespread overproduction of white wines, these innovations allowed winemakers to produce whites of real quality that are highly aromatic, have a good constitution, and can be conserved longer.

There is no precise definition of sweet *(moelleux)* white wines. These are wines that have a level of natural sugars of between 0.14 and 1.05 ounces per liter, while noble-rotted sweet *(liquoreux)* whites have a level of more than 1.05 ounces. Apart from some Entre-deux-Mers appellations, sweet whites wines are becoming increasingly rare in the Bordeaux region.

VINTAGES: MYTH OR REALITY?

Émile Peynaud, one of the leading oenologists in Bordeaux, says that "there are no bad vintages, only difficult vintages." The supposed quality of a vintage wine is a handy indicator for consumers, because it helps them to remember whether a particular year was "good" or "bad."

Today, however, the importance of the year is steadily decreasing, as is proven by Bordeaux wines. Nowadays, winegrowers and makers are less and less passive in the face of meteorological phenomena. At each stage of the vine's growth, then during the aging of the wine, they can intervene with increasing effectiveness to counterbalance the detrimental effects of cold, heat, rain, or drought. The research conducted for decades by different technical institutes in Bordeaux has been highly worthwhile.

In addition, the idea of a vintage applied to such a large area as the Bordeaux vineyards, or even only to some of the large parcels of land that make up the Bordeaux region, is practically senseless. It doesn't take into account the diversity of soils, microclimates, and especially the estates. The professionalization of wine producers has reached the point where high-quality wines can be made even under the most difficult circumstances. The "terrible" year of 1991, remembered for a freeze and for rain, still saw many vineyards produce very acceptable, and even some very good, wines.

This tulip-shaped glass has the official blessing of the INAO (Institut National des Appellations d'Origine.) Perfected by the institute, its shape is ideal for a successful tasting thanks to its capacity, the size of its base (held between the thumb and the index finger), and the tapering of the bowl, which helps concentrate the aromas.

REGIONAL APPELLATIONS

Nearly all the vineyards in the Bordeaux region are *appellations d'origine contrôlée,* a designation that guarantees their place of origin and standards of quality. The appellations can be divided into two main types. The first are local appellations, attached to a specific commune, such as Saint-Émilion, or a subregion like Médoc. The second are regional appellations that designate wines from the entire Bordeaux region that have certain characteristics in common, usually based on color. The Bordeaux and Bordeaux Supérieurs appellations include red wines, dry whites, rosés, and light reds, each with its own definition, grape varieties, and vinification methods.

The *Bordeaux de Marque* is a special case. These wines are the product of a merchant who assembles wines from different properties, producing a specific, consistent style from one year to another. Like all the wines of Bordeaux, Bordeaux de marque have the right to an *appellation d'origine contrôlée.*

These appellations are less prestigious than the local appellations, and often little known. They represent, however, a little more than half of the region's production and make an important contribution to the region's presence and name recognition in many markets. To some extent, the uniformity of their presentation disguises their wide diversity, and some lesser-known châteaux might provide surprisingly good value for the price paid.

Opposite: the stone bridge across the Garonne River in the heart of the city of Bordeaux. The city's name has become a general designation for all the wines produced within the Gironde department of France.

Bordeaux

In the 1980s, Louis Marinier used the slogan "the thousand and one châteaux of Bordeaux" to popularize this extended family, the largest Bordeaux appellation. In fact, there are nearly three thousand of these châteaux!

This large number of chateaux reflects the diversity of the wines carrying the appellation. Their differences are due not only to their various origins (the wines might come from areas with dissimilar soils and climates), but also to the growing and vinification techniques used on the different estates. Once produced mostly by merchants, Bordeaux red wines are now increasingly made on the estates—fifty-five percent at present. The designation "château" should no longer be taken literally, because it does not usually refer to buildings (which could be simple farm buildings), nor even to a particular vineyard (since an estate might expand by buying new parcels of land that are not adjacent to the original vineyard). What it does stand for is the wine itself, when it has been harvested, vinified, and bottled in the same production unit. The "château" is more or less a commercial brand name.

IDENTIFICATION

Type: red wine.

Grape varieties: merlot (45 percent), cabernet sauvignon (33 percent), cabernet franc (22 percent).

Area: 92,625 acres (1994).

Production: between 52.8 million and 66 million gallons on average.

Characteristics: Balanced, harmonious, elegant wines that are more fruity than full-bodied; can be drunk young.

Once described derogatorily as "petit Bordeaux," this appellation has improved in quality continuously over the past thirty years for a variety of reasons: the use of high-yield grape varieties and poor-quality soil has been phased out; yields have been limited to sixty-two hectoliters (1,637

gallons) per hectare (2.47 acres); and the approval committees that award *appellations d'origine contrôlées* to producers have become more professional.

That is not to say that everything is perfect. The price paid for this diversity is the continuing presence of too many mediocre wines that are weak in flavor and neutral in character. There is also the risk of finding poorly made wines that are unbalanced or have too high an alcohol content.

The other problem is that it is not always easy to find a likable Bordeaux because distribution circuits do not pay enough attention to the châteaux they sell from one year to the next. If you find a Bordeaux that you like, get in touch with its producer to make sure you will be able to find it again. The efforts that have been made to improve the quality of this appel-

lation have nonetheless had a noticeable effect and are leading to regular increases in sales, both in France and abroad.

A particularity of the Gironde is that there are wines with the Bordeaux appellation that might actually come from other appellations, such as Entre-deux-Mers or Sauternes, simply because these two appellations can only designate white wines. Some of the vintners in those areas also make red wines, and they are allowed to use the Bordeaux appellation. The inverse principle is also common with dry white wines produced in well-known

appellations like Saint-Émilion or Médoc taking the Bordeaux appellation.

A good Bordeaux has other characteristics in addition to its origin, grape varieties, and vinification methods. It should be light, easily digestible, and drinkable on any occasion. Bordeaux can be consumed fairly young (between one and two years), when they are very fresh, but many can stand up to longer aging of between five and ten years, which adds to their roundness and length in the mouth.

RICHELIEU'S HERBAL TEA

In the eighteenth century, the Duc de Richelieu, marshal of France, known as much for his dissolute lifestyle as for his bravery in combat, decided to spend the final days of his life in retirement in Aquitaine. He was a great lover of the wines of Bordeaux, and even claimed it reinvigorated him. The locals therefore dubbed Bordeaux wine "Richelieu's herbal tea" in honor of its supposed therapeutic qualities.

The Maison de la Qualité, in Beychac-et-Cailleau, was founded by its president,

Louis Marinier, in 1976, and expanded in 1986. It is a meeting place for the wine professionals and growers who grant the *appellations d'origine contrôlée,* but it is also open to the public. It provides information on Bordeaux and Bordeaux Supérieurs, and organizes vineyard tours for visitors. A new investment program initiated in 1996 will increase its activities, one of which will be a new space devoted to informing the public about the two appellations.

In Bordeaux, more than 22,000 winegrowers cultivate 247,000 acres of vineyards.

Bordeaux Supérieurs

Bordeaux Supérieurs are the finest Bordeaux. They come from the same geographic areas and are made from the same grape varieties, but they are considered to be of higher quality, especially in terms of their potential for aging. The AOC committee awards the Bordeaux Supérieur appellation to growers who decide to select part of their harvests and vinify it according to methode that assure this quality.

In its constant search for better quality, the Syndicat Viticole des Bordeaux et Bordeaux Supérieurs regularly revises its criteria, making them increasingly strict. They have introduced for aging criterion and now require that the approval committee taste the wine after the malolactic fermentation in order to better judge the wine's potential. The wine must stay in the cellar for at least a year after the harvest to ensure that it is close to its gustatory maturity and is capable of aging well.

After making these decisions, the vintners also implemented restrictions on the area and volume devoted to their Bordeaux Supérieurs. The maximum yield was fixed at fifty-nine hectoliters (1,558 gallons) per hectare (2.47 acres). These qualitative improvements have justified the raising of prices increased to the level of the côtes wines.

IDENTIFICATION

Type: red wine.

Grape varieties: merlot (45 percent), cabernet sauvignon (33 percent), cabernet franc (22 percent).

Area: 23,354 acres (1994).

Production: 11.9 million gallons on average.

Characteristics: Vinified so that it can be aged longer, this is a more well-rounded wine than red Bordeaux.

More and more vintners are starting to use new wood for aging, but this has provoked controversy. Some feel that in the case of wine produced from lower-quality terrain, the wood notes overpower the floral notes, which should remain the dominant quality of Bordeaux Supérieurs.

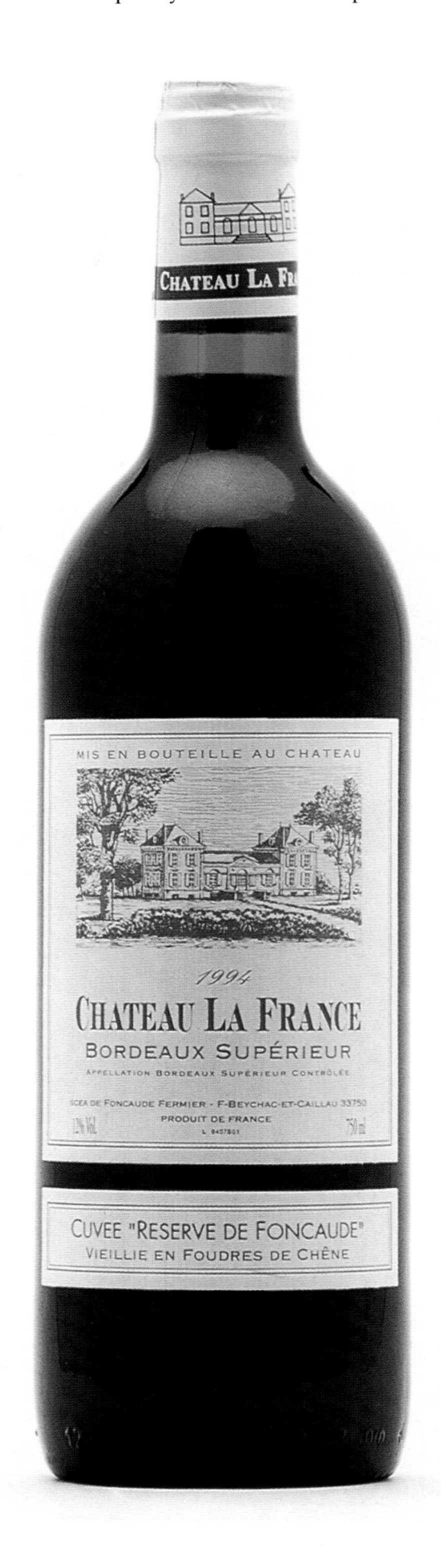

But, with quality raw materials (well-ripened grapes from old vines grown on quality terrain), there is no reason to avoid wood aging, which increases the complexity and harmony of the wine. Wood aging is also used for the small part of the harvest that becomes a *cuvée spéciale*

(also called a *cuvée réserve* or *cuvée sélection),* although this designation does not imply the use of new wood.

There are few stars in the constellation of Bordeaux Supérieurs, apart from perhaps those of Château Bonnet, which is also known for its Entre-deux-Mers whites. Wine lovers might want to look for Bordeaux Supérieurs that come from nobler territories, but for which the owners did not seek the local appellation. They might in this way find a wine from the Médoc or Saint-Émilion at a very reasonable price.

There are excellent wines to be found in this appellation at good prices, as long as the winemaker has respected the potential of his vineyard.

Bordeaux Rosés and Light Reds

Rosé is not one of the standouts of the Bordeaux region, and its production remains marginal in comparison with that of reds and whites, and is mostly destined for family consumption. Some estates use a small part of their harvest of red grape varieties to make a rosé because they want to offer a complete range of wine, or simply because they want to have some rosé on hand for hot summer nights.

IDENTIFICATION

Type: rosé wine.

Grape varieties: merlot (45 percent), cabernet sauvignon (33 percent), cabernet franc (22 percent).

Area: 3,668 acres (1994).

Production: 2.1 million gallons on average.

Characteristics: Lively and fruity, these wines are drunk young, which does not rule out some refined aromatic notes.

Several cooperatives specialize in the production of rosé wines, but no one in the region is attempting to compete with the rosés of Provence or the Loire Valley.

Rosé is made with black grapes. Their stems are removed, and they are crushed, pressed, and then vinified like white wine. There is no maceration with the skins and seeds. The tint of the wine ranges from pale salmon to a light red (like that of red currants or raspberries). The freshness and vivacity of rosés does not necessarily indicate a lack of noticeable aromatic notes, which make them an excellent accompaniment to a meal, especially in summer, or in any season when served with exotic foods.

The vinification method for light red wines, or clairets, is closer to that of red wine, but the must is left in contact with the skins for a shorter period of time, usually for around twenty-four hours. It is, in fact, a light-colored Bordeaux red, with a slightly more pronounced coloration than a rosé. In the eighteenth century, the name "claret" was used on the British market for Bordeaux wines. The clarets of that time were fairly light and fruity and were vinified rapidly. They were completely different from the highly colored and tannic wines of Burgundy and those of Porto, and quickly found fans in Great Britain. Even today, the term "claret" is often used to designate all the red wines of Bordeaux in British markets.

Today's clairets range in color from salmon to bright red, with a somewhat deeper coloration than rosés, and they have pronounced fruity aromas. The production of light reds is much lower than that of rosés.

Rosés and clairets should be drunk young, in the year following their harvest, to take advantage of their freshness and liveliness and their red-fruit aromas. While they can be produced throughout the Bordeaux appellation, their geographic origin is less important than it is for red Bordeaux—what counts is the vinification. The best are distinguished by their elegance and natural charm, and the producer is also important. (For clarets, Château Penin and Château Thieuley are notable.) One rarity is Rose de Loudenne, a rosé made from one hundred percent merlot grapes in the Médoc.

Sparkling Wines: Crémant-de-Bordeaux

The Crémant-de-Bordeaux appellation was created on April 3, 1990, validating a tradition that is at least a century old, although there has never been a very large production of this wine. Aging was accomplished in cellars and natural tunnels along the banks of the Garonne and Dordogne Rivers, which offered the ideal temperature and humidity for forming bubbles and aging the wine.

The creation of the *appellation d'origine contrôlée* followed the rules governing those for other French crémants. These rules are strict and are similar to those that control the wines of Champagne. The grapes must be picked by hand and the bottles stored on wire racks. The different phases of vinification are also clearly defined: pressing, fermentation control, bottle fermentation, riddling (turning of the bottles to settle out the sediments), and the disgorging of the plug of sediments. The wines used must come from the Bordeaux appellation, and the fermentation must also take place in the region.

Most Crémant-de-Bordeaux are processed as whites, with a very small production of rosé. They may be brut, demi-sec, or sweet depending on the amount of sugar added.

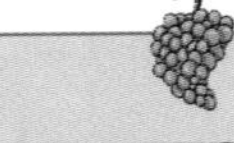

IDENTIFICATION

Type: sparkling white or rosé wine.

Grape varieties: all the traditional Bordeaux varieties, both red and white.

Area: 314 acres (1994).

Production: between 158,400 and 211,200 gallons on average.

Characteristics: Small, light bubbles; pale yellow or pink in color; fresh in the mouth, with fruity notes.

Although there have been definite improvements in quality since the creation of this appellation, Crémant-de-Bordeaux has not yet enjoyed commercial success. At the same time, production in other appellations (Loire, Alsace, Die, Limoux, etc.) has expanded quite spectacularly. Admittedly, Crémant-de-Bordeaux lacks the originality and specificity that would distinguish it from other sparkling wines. It is also difficult to convince consumers that "Bordeaux" can refer to a sparkling wine.

Dry White Bordeaux

The white grapes that are used to make dry white Bordeaux are crushed and pressed immediately after the harvest in order to separate the must from the skins and to avoid any maceration that might color the wine. The fermentation, which takes between twelve and fifteen days, is done at a temperature of between eighteen and twenty degrees Celsius. The winemaker usually avoids the second, or malolactic, fermentation in order to preserve the freshness of the wine. The aging period is fairly short so that the wine that can be drunk in the year following its harvest.

White wines are produced in all the Bordeaux appellations, the various regions and grape varieties yielding a wide range of styles. The Bordeaux appellation is increasingly taking precedence over the others; the appellation Haut-Bénauge, for example, a small region near Entre-deux-Mers, is used less and less by wine producers.

Nevertheless, the generic system of the appellation is not always clear to buyers and can be responsible for somewhat unfair competition. How can one distinguish between a basic dry white and one that is the product of a Médoc or Sauternes vineyard? Only true connoisseurs, capable of identifying a prestigious provenance hidden by the shared Bordeaux appellation, will be able to tell them apart.

Like Bordeaux reds, the dry whites have a Bordeaux Supérieur appellation, but it is rarely used because it applies to wines with a longer aging capacity, which is not what most winegrowers are seeking.

The dominant grape varieties are sémillon, which provides delicate perfumes and a rich texture; sauvignon blanc, for aromatic intensity and crispness; and muscadelle, which adds roundness to the whole. The increased use of sémillon can allow longer aging, but this practice is unusual. White wines are sometimes made exclusively with sauvignon grapes,

IDENTIFICATION

Type: white wine.

Grape varieties: sémillon (58 percent), sauvignon blanc (21 percent), muscadelle (10 percent), ugni blanc (9 percent), colombard (2 percent).

Area: 27,130 acres (1994).

Production: 14.5 million gallons on average.

Characteristics: Light, bright color; fruity and nervous, very fresh in the mouth; may have strong floral aromas.

which provide strong citrus aromas, but this is rare.

Floral aromas are the main characteristics of these wines. To reinforce this characteristic and also to conserve the wine's gustatory qualities for a longer period of time, the winegrowers' association for the appellation has asked that, beginning in 1999, the least aromatic grape varieties be ruled out.

During the past few years, oenological research has improved production techniques for dry whites. These include maceration with the skins, aging with fine lees, and fermentation in barrels, which emphasizes the aromas of the grapes, adds roundness and richness to the wine, and enables increased aging time. Overall, winemakers are following these guidelines more rigorously, and the general level of the appellation has improved, resulting in wines that are better made and that increasingly reflect the specific characteristics of their origin.

More than sixty percent of the dry white wines of Bordeaux are exported, and they remain relatively unknown in France. This means that their prices are fairly low, to the point where some winegrowers prefer to call them table wines, which are easier to sell.

Buyers can, however, find some excellent bottles, which make a perfect aperitif or an ideal accompaniment to shellfish and grilled fish. As with the reds, dry white wines from the most prestigious estates and appellations are available. There are some superb dry white wines from the Médoc and Sauternes that have benefitted from the care and expertise of experienced winegrowers.

The most famous is Pavillon Blanc, produced by Château Margaux. It is a pure sauvignon of great quality. The most legendary is the "Y" of Château d'Yquem, which is produced in very small quantities and only in certain years. It is characterized by an incomparable bouquet and great vigor.

THE BORDEAUX MERCHANT

The role of the Bordeaux merchant in the history of the wines of the region has always been just as important as that of the winegrower himself. It was the merchants, many of them British, who made a name for the region's wines and oriented production to respond to the demands of their customers.

Despite their name, Bordeaux merchants are not merely salespeople responsible for marketing the wines and guaranteeing the product's quality. They are also involved in the aging and bottling of the wines that they distribute under their own labels. Today, there are more than three hundred such brand names. They are selective blends of wines (red, white, or rosé) from the different Bordeaux areas.

The Bordeaux trading houses (which number around four hundred) sell more than 600 million bottles, making them a powerful economic force. They bottle around 132 million gallons of wine and store some 66 million gallons. This enables them to play a regulatory role in the market by providing a cushion against major fluctuations in prices.

During the nineteenth century, the merchant was practically the only seller of wines, and he often aged the wine himself. Only a few prestigious châteaux were able to make and bottle their wines themselves, but even they left the selling to the merchants. In 1850, there were only about fifty wineries that were designated châteaux. Today, there are around five thousand.

The term "château" may seem confusing, but it does have a precise definition. The wine carrying the name of a château must come from an independent operation that produces, ages, and bottles its own wine. The wine can, however, be sold by an outside merchant. Since World War II, more and more estate owners have understood the advantages of selling their wines themselves, especially on the French market, even though this means that they spend more on prospecting, canvassing, and advertising. Also, aside from interest in their own labels, merchants are becoming less involved in the aging of estate wines, since progress in oenological techniques has enabled the winegrowers to ensure a high level of quality.

Today, Bordeaux merchants retain an important role in exporting wine, an activity they have been practicing since their beginnings. Thanks to their networks, some of them a century old, they now handle more than 80 percent of Bordeaux exports to about sixty countries. This activity represents a turnover of nearly four billion French francs (645 million U.S. dollars.) A volume of this size could not possibly come from just the most prestigious châteaux; it is made up of all Bordeaux wines, one-third of whose total production of between 47.5 million and 52.8 million gallons is exported.

The demands of modern commerce have led to the growing concentration of Bordeaux trading houses. Currently, some thirty companies account for eighty-five percent of turnover in the sector, and the ten leading companies account for nearly half!

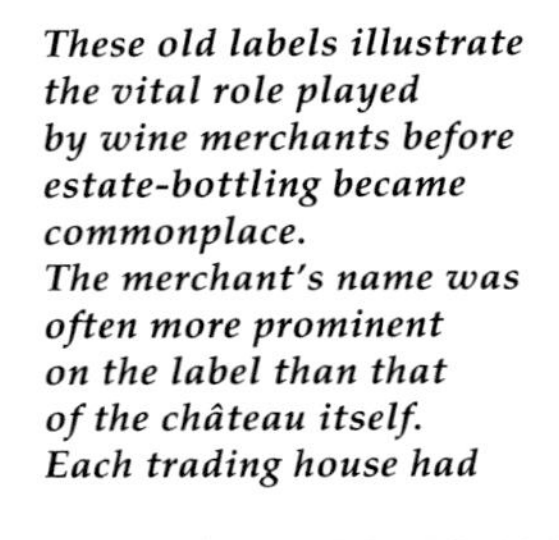

These old labels illustrate the vital role played by wine merchants before estate-bottling became commonplace. The merchant's name was often more prominent on the label than that of the château itself. Each trading house had

a reputation based on its expertise in the aging and bottling of wines. Wines from the same estate did not necessarily have the same value, as it would depend upon which merchant had bottled it. One bottler with an excellent reputation was Nicolas. With its extensive retail distribution, it had a vested interest in ensuring its good name.

Today, only pleasure boats arrive at the Bordeaux quays. All commercial activities have been transferred to Verdon. To the right of the Bourse du Commerce is the famous quai des Chartrons, and, on the left, the quai de Paludate. Most of the large trading companies of Bordeaux had, and still have, their headquarters on these two quays.

Represented by two professional associations, the merchants play a vital role, along with the winegrowers' associations, in the Conseil interprofessionnel des vins de Bordeaux. Created in 1918 as the Union de la propriété et du commerce and renamed in 1948, the CIVB is charged with harmonizing the sometimes divergent interests of the sector, especially with regard to the prices of wine and, in a general sense, the direction and regulation of the markets. It has a large annual budget of 120 million French francs (19.5 million U.S. dollars). This is mostly spent on a variety of promotional activities in France and abroad, but is also used for market analyses, various training programs involving Bordeaux, and the research conducted by the Institut d'œnologie de Bordeaux.

COOPERATIVE CAVES

Cooperatives appeared in the 1930s in response to the crisis that had recently struck the Bordeaux vineyards. By banding together, small and large winegrowers could better exploit their estates while building up stocks that allowed them some leverage in years with poor sales.

Gradually, these cooperatives developed primarily into means through which winegrowers worked to improve quality at all levels of production and to promote sales in most markets. There are currently fifty-four cooperatives in thirty-six of the fifty-seven Bordeaux appellations. They do not enjoy the same prestige as the great estates and do not have the recognition from which the powerful merchants profit. But their economic importance is undeniable, thanks to the volume of wine that they vinify and stock. With six thousand members, they currently manage twenty-six percent of the region's vines and account for thirty-eight percent of harvest declarations. This represents nearly 39.6 million gallons, or one in four bottles of Bordeaux.

Bordeaux de marque

For a long time, Bordeaux merchants only sold wine made by others. Unlike their counterparts in Champagne, they began selling wine under their own labels at a relatively late date, which explains why these wines are still rather unknown today.

For consumers, a Bordeaux means a château wine, and the merchants themselves contributed to this belief. Under their own labels, they sell an assemblage of wines from different origins that are of great quality. While faithful to their origins in Bordeaux, the wines express the specific style of the merchants who create them. Consumers know by the label that they are buying a quality wine with a consistent taste.

This system of consistency from year to year contradicts the vintage concept, which is so crucial to the character of Bordeaux wines. But, although some *Bordeaux de marque* are vintages, many buyers prefer above all a consistency of style to the annual ups and downs caused by climatic fluctuations.

- Malesan, from William Pitters. A best-seller in France, with highly consistent quality.
- Mouton-Cadet. Made by the merchant company Baron Philippe de Rothschild, it has profited from the fame of Mouton-Rothschild to the point where it has become a veritable ambassador for Bordeaux wines around the world. This is a textbook case that some purists find shocking. With a fine texture and a good capacity for aging, Mouton-Cadet has given birth to a whole range of red, white, and rosé wines that benefit from the same prestige.
- Numéro 1, from Dourthe. The first product of this house was a dry white that made waves with its aromatic intensity, a result of the revolution in white Bordeaux that occurred in the 1980s. The range has since been rounded out with several other wines, including a fruity red. Under the label Beau-Mayne, the house also sells a more classic range that is of equally high quality.
- Maître d'Estournel. Like Mouton-Cadet, this generic label benefits from the fame of a prestigious château. The result is an honorable Bordeaux.
- Beau-Rivage, from Borie-Manoux. This wine is distinguished by its balance and good capacity for aging (five years or more), longer than most generic wines.
- Yvecourt, the standard label of the merchant Yvon Mau. It comes in several types, all of them highly consistent.

• 1725, from Barton & Guestier, a subsidiary of the Seagram group. The top exporter of Bordeaux sells a range of high-quality wines under this label, whose name refers to the date of the founding of the company.

• Collection Privée, from Cordier. This includes a fine white made mostly with sauvignon grapes. The range includes one wine for each major Bordeaux appellation.

• Calvet Tradition, from a well-known company. A fruity, aromatic wine and a good reflection of Bordeaux expertise.

• Ginestet. This excellent red Bordeaux uses the name of the production company and is in the great tradition of the Bordeaux merchant/winegrowers.

• Kressmann Monopole. This was the first Bordeaux de marque, created in 1912 by Édouard Kressman. The current product remains faithful to its origins.

THE MÉDOC

The Médoc, the most prestigious winegrowing region in the world, developed over a period of nearly four hundred years into what it is today. North of Bordeaux along the Gironde estuary on a strip of earth six miles wide and fifty miles long, the area enjoys a mild, humid climate that is fairly stable, although there can be great variations from one year to another. Long covered with forests and thus unsuitable for the growing of crops, its soil of gravel, clay, and sand was ideal for winegrowing; the roots of the vine are forced to "suffer" by reaching deep into the soil for the water and other elements they need, which will end up concentrated in the grape.

Historically, Médoc is not the oldest Bordeaux winegrowing region—far from it—but it quickly made up for lost time. With the classification of 1855, it was the first to establish a qualitative ranking of its most important estates.

The area is divided into two zones: Médoc, to the north, and Haut Médoc, which runs from the communities of Saint-Seurin-de-Cadourne and Vertheuil to Blanquefort, near Bordeaux. The former zone does not include specific appellations but has *crus bourgeois* of excellent quality. Haut Médoc, on the other hand, encompasses six local appellations that are among the most prestigious of the Bordeaux region: Margaux, Moulis, Listrac-Médoc, Saint-Julien, Pauillac, and Saint-Estèphe.

While the Médoc is confined to a narrow strip of land, the Gironde estuary offers it an opening to the rest of the world; this geography reflects the dual character of Aquitaine, which is both reserved and introverted yet open to the world. The same could be said of the region's highly concentrated wines, which are exported around the world.

Left: Château Cos d'Estournel, one of the most unusual buildings in the Médoc.
Above: a small wooden statue of Saint Vincent, the patron saint of winegrowers, from the chai *of Château Lascombes in Margaux.*

Médoc

In theory, all Médoc vineyards have the right to the Médoc appellation, but in practice, it is used only for the lower part of the region. The demarcation line, defined by usage rather than legislation, runs to the north of Saint-Seurin-de-Cadourne and Vertheuil.

Here the landscape gradually changes, flattening out, with the gravelly hilltops characteristic of Haut Médoc gradually disappearing. The farther north you go, the fewer vineyards you see. They disappear completely to the north of Saint-Vivien, where they are replaced by a landscape and climate typical of the seaside.

Palus, the local name for the recent alluvial soil and marshy areas found near rivers, is more common here. When wines from these areas are perfectly vinified, they can be generous and open.

As for grape varieties, there are hardly any differences between those of Médoc and Haut Médoc, aside from the fact that merlot is slightly more common in

IDENTIFICATION

Type: red wine.

Grape varieties: cabernet sauvignon (54 percent), merlot (40 percent), cabernet franc (6 percent).

Area: 11,577 acres (1994).

Production: 6.9 million gallons on average.

Characteristics: These deep red wines have a fruity bouquet and are well rounded. Some can reach great refinement, with excellent tannic richness.

The tower of the Château La Tour de By, a Médoc **cru bourgeois.** *This former lighthouse overlooks the vineyard and was built in 1825 on the ruins of a flour mill.*

Médoc, lending more roundness to the wine. It also matures faster, so the wines can be drunk sooner.

The châteaux are less opulent in the Médoc, and there are more cooperatives. As the soil gets richer, with more silt and fewer pebbles and less sand, the quality of the wines decreases. Nevertheless, a large volume of wine is produced here, slightly more than in Haut Médoc.

This district does not have local appellations or crus classés, but it boasts some very good *crus bourgeois* (see box on page 51), which often benefit from the particular conditions of a few isolated gravelly hilltops. This is true of Loudenne, La Tour de By, and Le Boscq, whose names are better known than some *crus classés*. At one time there existed a curious classification called *crus artisans*, but it has today thankfully fallen out of use.

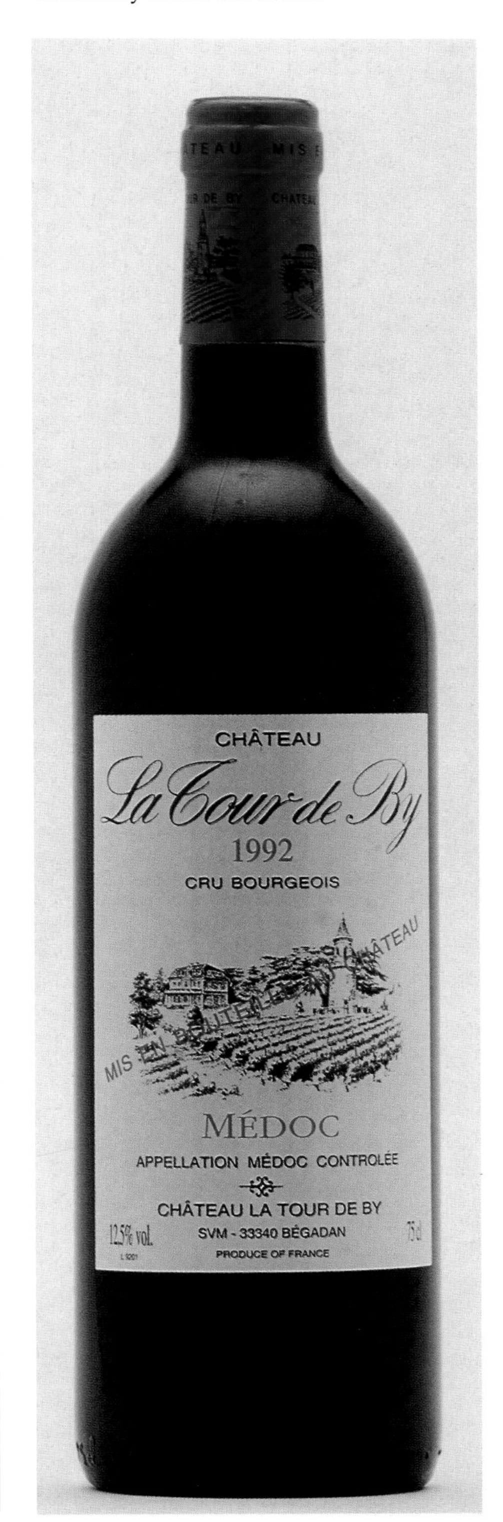

Much of the production of Médoc is used by merchants to make wine under their own labels. But there are also many estates that produce highly appreciated wines: Escot, Patache d'Aux, Les Ormes Sorbet, Rollan de By, Tour Haut-Caussan,

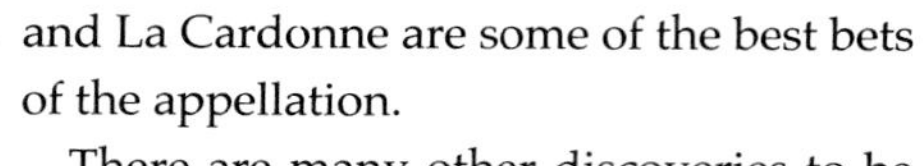

and La Cardonne are some of the best bets of the appellation.

There are many other discoveries to be made here, even though there are also many irregularities, such as wines lacking in body or concentration.

WINE LABELS

The label, cork, and sealing cap are the three elements of a bottle's presentation.

While it may have aesthetic appeal, the presentation should also, and above all, be informative. Things have changed a great deal since the days when there were no laws governing the matter, and winegrowers were content to choose a pre-printed label like the one shown below from a catalogue. This label dates from the nineteenth century.

The current regulations have three

main goals: to inform the buyer as thoroughly as possible while avoiding anything that might be misleading; to identify the parties responsible for the contents of the bottle in case of problems, and to allow the promotion of the product through the use of the brand name.

Says Claude Clévenot, founder of the Imprimerie du Clos du Moulin and a well-known label designer, "While a wine can easily be misidentified during a blind tasting, it would be unpardonable if any misunderstandings arose from looking at the label."

VINES AND ROSES

It is not unusual to see beautiful rose bushes at the end of rows of vines all over the Médoc. They are there not for aesthetic reasons, but rather because they once served as an alarm signal to winegrowers: the roses fall prey to disease before the vines do, warning the growers to start treatment of the vines.

Haut Médoc

It wasn't until the second half of the sixteenth century that vines appeared in the Médoc, although they had already been cultivated for some time in Aquitaine. This dry area with poor soil had been covered by forests until the Middle Ages, when rye fields were planted around the first monastic parishes and estates.

The gradual growth of the port of Bordeaux, which handled wines from Graves and Entre-deux-Mers, prompted investors to take a closer look at the region located just to the north of the city. At first, only "clarets," which can be drunk during the year following their harvest, were produced in the area. A favorite with British customers, they were expected to be "good, pure, clean, new, and sellable." A change came at the end of the seventeenth century, when wine lovers began to seek out more refined, sophisticated wines. Techniques like the topping-off of the barrels to compensate for evaporation and the use of better-quality barrels were introduced. At the same time, the geographic provenance of the wine and even the names of some estates, such as Latour and Lafite, began to appear in the commercial documents.

IDENTIFICATION

Type: red wine.

Grape varieties: cabernet sauvignon (54 percent), merlot (40 percent), cabernet franc (6 percent).

Area: 10,278 acres (1994).

Production: 5.8 million gallons on average.

Characteristics: These deep red wines are generous without being overpowering. They have great finesse and are very smooth when young. Their robust structure enables long aging that can produce remarkable wines.

The real "viticultural colonization" of the Médoc began in the eighteenth century. Bordeaux merchants and estate owners began to plant vines on the great estates, which were managed by their stewards. As the quality of the wine improved, so did its reputation.

The practices used at the time, however, differ greatly from those of today. Between one-fifth and one-tenth of an estate was planted with white grape varieties, but the entire yield of both black and white grapes was thrown into the same vat. It was also common to employ the *travail à l'anglaise,* or "English method," which was the practice of mixing the harvests of poor years with stronger wines from Cahors, Roussillon, and even Spain.

Gradually, a hierarchy based on selling

WINE LABELS

This delightful label was used in the 1930s, when it was fashionable to include a black-and-white photograph of the château on the label. The information about the origins of the wine furnished on the label does not go very far. Like the majority of wines at the time—both those produced in Bordeaux and those shipped from the port of Bordeaux—they are identified only as "Bordeaux." This practice was not unique to the wines of Château Larose-Trintaudon, but was also used by the merchants. There were still no laws at the time regulating *appellations contrôlées.*

prices was established. This was the work of the wine brokers, who acted as intermediaries between the Bordeaux winegrowers and merchants, and who played a determining role in the fixing of prices based on fluctuations in supply and demand.

Over a period of thirty years, the registers of Abraham Lawton, one of the earliest known wine brokers, who operated in the second half of the eighteenth century, showed a strong trend: the prices of the wines of Médoc (and those of Haut-Brion) continued to climb.

In spite of the technical problems of the period, it was becoming clear that the region's wines were worth far more when they were aged for longer periods of time in barrels. There were, however, great risks of accident or loss, and the cost of investment was high. Showing no small

amount of courage, the Médoc estate owners, with the help of the merchants, nevertheless took their chances.

This marked the "advent of quality": the top specialists became aware of the correlation between the natural environment and the quality of a wine. In addition, technical improvements were being made at every stage of winemaking, from the harvest to barrel-aging, and an increasing amount of care went into the entire process.

In May 1787, Thomas Jefferson, the future president of the United States, spent a few days in Aquitaine. Fascinated by wines and winegrowing techniques, he met with the top experts of Bordeaux. The notes he made during his visit represent the first serious attempt to rank the wines of Médoc by *cru* and by estate.

At the beginning of the nineteenth century, wine professionals were already referring to a hierarchy of Médoc *crus* that included the best estates, whose wines were sold at much higher prices than others, mostly on export markets. In 1855, an official ranking made during the Exposition Universelle in Paris would confirm this classification (see page 50). It has been changed only once since then, in 1973, with the promotion of Mouton-Rothschild to the rank of *premier cru*. Thus, nearly a century ahead of the other Bordeaux districts, the Médoc established a classification of its best *crus*.

Between 1935 and 1950, the system of *appellations contrôlées* reinforced this hierarchy by distinguishing six local appellations within Haut Médoc. Today, some people contest the classification of 1855, which they feel no longer reflects reality when it comes to the quality of the wines. It is true that the tasting of some *crus bourgeois* often leads to wonderful discoveries —testimony to the success of a few passionate winegrowers—but, until now, with the exception of the precedent set in 1973, the professionals concerned have not been willing to question the decisions made by their predecessors in 1855.

The quality of the wines of Haut Médoc results from the combination of several factors. These include the sand, gravel, and clay soil; the occasional sunny hilltop; and the excellent drainage, which forces the vine's roots to dig deeper into the earth to find water, helping it to develop its special properties.

The climate, primarily oceanic because of its proximity to the Atlantic and the Gironde estuary, is temperate, although bad freezes are not unusual in the springtime.

Above all, it is the contribution of the men and women of the region that explains the quality and the reputation of the Haut Médoc. Over the centuries, the growers of the Médoc have continually worked at improving their vines, managing to stay ahead of other winegrowing areas. They were able to coax unequaled expression out of their cabernet sauvignon grapes, complemented by the roundness and sweetness of the merlot grapes.

In addition to its ranked *crus* and the six local appellations, the Haut Médoc has lesser-known, but high-quality wines. They consistently exemplify the "taste of Bordeaux"—wines that are a pleasure to drink, never heavy, with appealing aromatic variations and a great deal of finesse. Their tannic structure, which is both dense and elegant, and their balance make long aging possible. On the other hand, these wines can also be enjoyed young. They simply never disappoint.

THE CLASSIFICATION OF 1855

Napoleon III, newly arrived in power, decided in 1855 to organize an Exposition Universelle in Paris to show off the riches of France to the rest of the world. Agricultural products, including wine, were the stars of the show, and the prefectures of the country's departments were invited to send samples of their best products.

In the Médoc, this request created an uproar. The makers of the *grands crus,* already aware of their superior quality, did not want to see their products mixed up with the less famous wines of the Gironde. Thus was born the idea of sending these wines to Paris under a special banner that would set them apart.

The Bordeaux Chamber of Commerce asked several wine brokers to establish a classification, based simply on the selling prices of the wines registered in their archives during the past century. There were no competitive tastings, just the comparison among professionals of the international value of the wines. The rating system was divided into two parts: red wines, themselves divided into five categories, and white wines, divided into three categories. In fact, only the reds of Médoc (plus Haut-Brion in Graves) and the *liquoreux* whites of Sauternes and Barsac were included.

In 1954, the Institut national des appellations d'origine classified the wines of Saint-Émilion. This ranking is revised every ten years. In 1959, the wines of Graves were classified.

In 1973, more than a century after the 1855 classification, the authorities decided to review the ranking of the wines of the Médoc, but this proposal caused such an uproar that the review never occurred. Only Mouton-Rothschild, thanks to the relentless lobbying of its owner, was elevated to the top classification.

Often disparaged by professionals as having only historical value, the 1855 classification has not been overhauled since it was formulated. Its revision would no doubt involve too many difficulties for anyone who undertook to change this historic monument.

PREMIERS CRUS

- Lafite-Rothschild (Pauillac)
- Latour (Pauillac)
- Margaux (Margaux)
- Mouton-Rothschild (Pauillac)
- Haut-Brion (Graves)

SECONDS CRUS

- Brane-Cantenac (Margaux)
- Cos d'Estournel (Saint-Estèphe)
- Ducru-Beaucaillou (Saint-Julien)
- Durfort-Vivens (Margaux)
- Gruaud-Larose (Saint-Julien)
- Lascombes (Margaux)
- Léoville-Las-Cases (Saint-Julien)
- Léoville-Poyferré (Saint-Julien)
- Léoville-Barton (Saint-Julien)
- Montrose (Saint-Estèphe)
- Pichon-Longueville-Baron (Pauillac)
- Pichon-Longueville-Comtesse-de-Lalande (Pauillac)
- Rausan-Ségla (Margaux)
- Rauzan-Gassies (Margaux)

Troisièmes crus

- Boyd-Cantenac (Margaux)
- Cantenac-Brown (Margaux)
- Calon-Ségur (Saint-Estèphe)
- Desmirail (Margaux)
- Ferrière (Margaux)
- Giscours (Margaux)
- d'Issan (Margaux)
- Kirwan (Margaux)
- Lagrange (Saint-Julien)
- La Lagune (Haut Médoc)
- Langoa (Saint-Julien)
- Malescot-Saint-Exupéry (Margaux)
- Marquis d'Alesme-Becker (Margaux)
- Palmer (Margaux)

Quatrièmes crus

- Beychevelle (Saint-Julien)
- Branaire-Ducru (Saint-Julien)
- Duhart-Milon-Rothschild (Pauillac)
- Lafon-Rochet (Saint-Estèphe)
- Marquis-de-Terme (Margaux)
- Pouget (Margaux)
- Prieuré-Lichine (Margaux)
- Saint-Pierre (Saint-Julien)
- Talbot (Saint-Julien)
- La Tour-Carnet (Haut Médoc)

Cinquièmes crus

- Batailley (Pauillac)
- Belgrave (Haut Médoc)
- Camensac (Haut Médoc)
- Cantemerle (Haut Médoc)
- Clerc-Milon (Pauillac)
- Cos-Labory (Saint-Estèphe)
- Croizet-Bages (Pauillac)
- Dauzac (Margaux)
- Grand-Puy-Ducasse (Pauillac)
- Grand-Puy-Lacoste (Pauillac)
- Haut-Bages-Libéral (Pauillac)
- Haut-Batailley (Pauillac)
- Lynch-Bages (Pauillac)
- Lynch-Moussas (Pauillac)
- Pédesclaux (Pauillac)
- Pontet-Canet (Pauillac)
- d'Armailhac (Pauillac)
- du Tertre (Margaux)

CRUS BOURGEOIS

The term *cru bourgeois* was once commonly used for properties acquired by the middle-class (bourgeois) families of Bordeaux. After the 1855 classification, the Médoc became a fashionable winegrowing area, and every well-off family wanted to own a vacation cottage and a vineyard there.

Following the classification of the *grands crus,* a different classification appeared to help the numerous Médoc properties distinguish themselves from the others. First the wine brokers, at the request of the Chamber of Commerce, made a selection of *crus bourgeois* in 1932. It included three rankings: *crus bourgeois supérieurs exceptionnels* (6), *crus bourgeois supérieurs* (99), and *crus bourgeois* (339).

In 1972, the classification was revised by the Syndicat des crus bourgeois, which came up with three categories: *crus exceptionnels, crus grand bourgeois,* and *crus bourgeois.* Luckily, these categories were not accepted by the European Community, which authorized only the identification *cru bourgeois* on the label.

Today, there are 282 *crus bourgeois* in the Médoc, divided among the eight appellations. They represent about fifty percent of the total production of the district. Because of their great number and the absence of classification, the term *cru bourgeois* does not have much meaning and does not really serve as a guide for buyers. Both exceptional and ordinary wines can have the same designation, and there are even some *crus bourgeois* that are considered far superior to certain *crus classés.* Examples of top-notch *crus bourgeois* are Sociando-Mallet, Haut-Marbuzet, and Phélan-Ségur. Those who take the trouble to look may find some excellent wines in this category, and at very good prices.

Margaux

Margaux refers to a town, an appellation, a ranked *premier cru,* and one of the most handsome châteaux in the Médoc. It is also one of the most famous wines in the world. Compared with the virile, austere wines of Pauillac, the wines of Margaux have an almost feminine charm and an elegant finesse. Coincidentally, Château Margaux, the best-known *cru* (see pages 56-57), has often been directed by women.

The fame of Château Margaux, however, should not overshadow the other great estates of this appellation, which is the largest in the Haut Médoc. It encompasses five villages: Margaux, Cantenac, Soussans, Labarde, and Arsac, and no less than twenty-one of its *crus* were included the 1855 classification, the record in Médoc for one appellation.

The depth of the layer of sand and gravel is the primary characteristic of the soil, but the diversity of the wines produced there is also the result of the existence of a series of gravelly hilltops, separated by valleys filled with little streams. Even more than the soil, however, it is the talent of man that has made the difference in quality, perhaps even more so here than in other regions. It is an incontestable fact that better wines are produced on some estates than on others, even though the terrain is similar. Another proof is that, during the four centuries that wine has been made in Margaux, some *crus* have enjoyed a great fame that is hardly justified today, and there are *crus* that were ranked in 1855 that are nowhere near the quality of some *crus bourgeois.*

The village church in Margaux, next to Château Margaux.

IDENTIFICATION

Type: red wine.

Grape varieties: cabernet sauvignon (54 percent), merlot (40 percent), cabernet franc (6 percent).
Area: 3,312 acres (1994).

Production: 1.9 million gallons on average.

Characteristics: Finesse and suppleness are the principal qualities of these wines. They have particular aromatic characteristics—notably, violets and spices, and a remarkable potential for aging capacity.

There is another side to the finesse and elegance of Margaux. Some wines are too thin, lacking in real body and substance, and do not age well. Cabernet sauvignon grapes are king here, and, in the best *crus,* they account for a larger proportion than in the average wines of the appellation. The sweetness of the merlot grape and its faster maturation are less sought-after in the Margaux style.

Aging is indispensable to the blossoming of these wines. The strict minimum is five years, and ten to fifteen years is a reasonable range. To bring out the best of their qualities, the finest *crus* should be aged even longer to ensure that their tannins are completely dissolved into a harmony that can reach true excellence.

This appellation is near the city of Bordeaux, and Margaux is worth a detour, not only for its wine, but also for the diversity of its landscapes and the style of its châteaux. The following is a selective list of estates.

• Cantenac-Brown. An English painter, John-Lewis Brown, designed this neo-Tudor château, a surprising sight in Aquitaine. Commissioned by the merchant Armand Lalande, it was a society meeting place at the end of the nineteenth century. Originally, the estate included Boyd-Cantenac, which was separated from it in 1860.

• Dauzac. It was here and at Ducru-Beaucaillou that experiments were conducted with *la bouillie bordelaise* (a mixture of copper sulfate, chalk, and water), which conquered downy mildew. Now run by André Lurton, the vineyard is coming back into favor with wine experts.

• Desmirail. Famous in the nineteenth century and ranked as a *troisième cru* in the 1855 classification, the estate later nearly disappeared after being cut into parcels. However the tenacity of Lucien Lurton, who little by little bought back the original estate, has led to its renaissance.

• Durfort-Vivens. In addition to its aristocratic origins (it was owned by the powerful Durfort de Duras family, then by the Vicomte de Vivens), the estate carries the prestige of having been applauded by Thomas Jefferson. Fluctuations in sales later led to the loss of many of its

vines. Once again, Lucien Lurton has come to the rescue, resuscitating the estate and bringing luster back to the wines.

• Ferrière. In area, this is the smallest (11.1 acres) of the ranked vineyards. Located in the heart of Margaux, it is encircled by a wall, a rarity in the Gironde. Managed for a long time by the owners of Lascombes, it has found new style and quality since being acquired by the Merlaut family.

• Giscours. Giscours was abandoned during the period between the two world wars. Since the 1950s, it has been completely revived by the Tari family, which has made it into an exemplary estate. The vineyard is known as much for its promotion of polo as for its wine.

• Issan. The seventeenth-century manor house is harmoniously beautiful, and so is the finesse of its wine. The Cruse family

has made this a cultural crossroads in the Bordeaux region.

• Kirwan. Around 1880, this estate was provided with a train station to make it easily accessible to visitors—it belonged to the mayor of Bordeaux at the time. While the name comes from one of its Irish owners, the property currently belongs to the Schröder et Schyler company, Bordeaux merchants for seven generations.

• Labégorce-Zédé. A perfect example of the level of quality that can be achieved by a well-made *cru bourgeois*, this wine easily rivals higher-ranked crus.

• Lascombes. For a long time, this was just a small estate with a few acres of vineyards. It has since been greatly expanded by Alexis Lichine and the British Bass-Charrington group. Parcels of its land are located throughout the appellation, and the estate boasts the latest vinification equipment.

• Marquis de Terme. Distinguished by a fairly large proportion of merlot (thirty-five percent), this 86.5-acre estate produces a Margaux that is perfectly typical of the appellation.

• Palmer. Named after an English major who served in Wellington's army, this château with elegant turrets was built at the end of the nineteenth century. The estate produces one of the most representative and consistent Margaux in the appellation.

• Prieuré-Lichine. On the site of a former priory dating to the end of the middle ages, this estate owes everything to the sorely missed Alexis Lichine, who completely rebuilt it beginning in 1951 and made it into one of the leading lights of the appellation and a popular tourist destination.

• Rausan-Ségla. This estate was created in the seventeenth century, when it was already known as one of the greats. Although it was separated from Rauzan-Gassies a century later, it is still one of the best in Margaux. Its recent purchase by the Wertheimer family (owners of Chanel) inaugurated a new era of quality.

• Siran. This estate belongs to the Miailhe family, which played an important role in the history of Margaux and of the Bordeaux region in general. Many wine experts feel that its *cru bourgeois* deserved to be rated as a *cru classé*.

CHÂTEAU MARGAUX

The origins of this estate go back to at least the seventeenth century, when the lands of La Mothe belonged to the Albret family. Beginning in the fifteenth century, a series of La Mothe-Margaux barons passed through, followed by other great names from the past, such as the Montferrands, Thomas de Durfort, Jean Gimel (a Bordeaux merchant), and the Lory family.

For a time, Margaux was linked to Haut-Brion through the marriage in 1654 of the daughter of Arnaud de Pontac, owner of the famous Graves vineyard, to the heir to the Aulède family, owners of Margaux. The first high-quality grape varieties were planted around 1750. The wine's fame spread quickly, and a steward named Berlon is said to have made many improvements in vinification at the end of the seventeenth century.

The estate fell into the hands of the Fumel family at the beginning of the eighteenth century. They continued its expansion, but then the property was confiscated and pillaged during the French Revolution. Laure de Fumel, the last person to carry the family name, later bought back the estate, and then married Hector de Brane, who owned Mouton and Brane-Cantenac. The marriage didn't last, however, and Laure was forced to sell Margaux to the Marquis de la Colonilla. In 1810, he built the classically elegant château that still stands today, along with the small village that surrounds it. They were designed by the architect Louis Combes, a student of Victor Louis, who designed Bordeaux's Grand Théâtre. Combes's building replaced an ancient fortified citadel dating to the middle ages.

Sometimes poorly managed, Margaux later passed through the hands of several owners before becoming the property of Count Pillet-Will, governor of the Banque de France. In 1921, its management was taken over by a company of which the merchant house Ginestet was at first majority shareholder and then full owner in 1949.

In 1977, the estate was sold to André Mentzelopoulos, the owner of the Félix Potin chain of grocery stores. He was then at the pinnacle of his fortunes, and the news made a big splash. When he

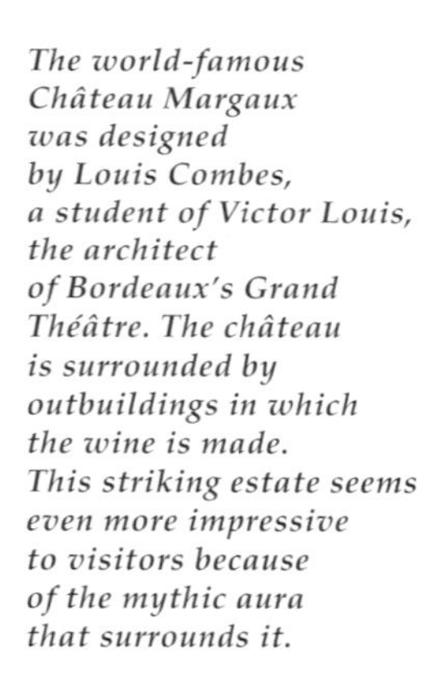

The world-famous Château Margaux was designed by Louis Combes, a student of Victor Louis, the architect of Bordeaux's Grand Théâtre. The château is surrounded by outbuildings in which the wine is made. This striking estate seems even more impressive to visitors because of the mythic aura that surrounds it.

died three years later, his widow, and later his daughter, took over and succeeded in completely refurbishing the estate and bringing it back to the top of the appellation. They were not the first women to play an important role in the management of the Château Margaux.

Today, vines cover 245 acres of the 647-acre estate, including 29.6 acres of white varieties, exclusively sauvignon. The mix of varieties is seventy-five percent cabernet sauvignon, twenty percent merlot, and five percent Petit-Verdot. Average production is 350,000 bottles of red and 40,000 of white (sold under the label Pavillon Blanc). The second wine of Château Margaux is called Pavillon Rouge. This well-tended estate is managed by the charming Paul Pontallier.

How has Château Margaux managed to maintain its pre-eminence over a period of three centuries? The estate's soils certainly have much to do with it, as do unceasing efforts of the owners to perfect the wines and make them the best possible representatives of the appellation. With their powerful, seductive aromas, these wines are immediately appealing, but it takes a long period of aging (a minimum of ten to fifteen years) before they best express their character.

Robert Parker, the American Bordeaux specialist, says that the 1990 Château Margaux reminds him of the great 1953 Château Margaux, with a weight that is comparable to 1982 and an amazing presence in the mouth. He describes the flowery bouquet as "sublime," with notes of black currant, smoke, new oak, and Oriental spices. In the mouth, he finds the tannins tender and the wine expansive, remarkably refined, rich, with a finish that is "as smooth as silk." He concludes that the 1990 Château Margaux is the most classic that has been produced by the Mentzelopoulos family and that one of the great vintages, it has a highly promising future ahead of it, according to Parker.

Margaux has its own cooperage, located in the Cour des Artisans, which also houses all the equipment necessary for the cultivation of the vines and the upkeep of the property.

Listrac

Like its sister and neighbor, Moulis, which is not, however, its twin, Listrac is the most continental of the Médoc appellations. The climate here is rougher than it is along the Gironde estuary, sometimes resulting in terrible frosts in winter and spring. In addition, the differences in maturity between the merlots and the cabernets sauvignons make the work of the winegrowers more difficult.

The soil is mostly made up of a mixture of sand and gravel, with the exception of predominantly clay-limestone soil in the center (on the Médrac plateau). Merlot is more important here than in other appellations. Listrac (which means "on the edge of"—probably in reference to the nearby forests) obtained an *appellation d'origine contrôlée* in 1953 that is limited to the area of the Listrac-Médoc community. This tardy recognition is a reminder that this is a somewhat forgotten appellation of the Médoc. None of its châteaux were listed in the classification of 1855.

Vines cover the whole area, and there are plenty of well-made, reasonably priced *crus bourgeois* that are favorites with many wine lovers. Examples are Clarke (owned by Edmond de Rothschild), Fourcas-Dupré, Fourcas-Hosten (located in the heart of a beautiful park that is famous for its cyclamens), Fourcas-Loubaney, Lestage, and others. "Real" winegrowers like the Gobinauds—owners of their own vines and not just employees of an insurance company or a financial group—can still be found in Listrac. The increase in the appellation's quality has led to the creation of new vineyards like Mayne-Lalande, and the district has a cooperative that produces Grand Listrac and La Caravelle, a *cuvée de prestige*.

IDENTIFICATION

Type: red wine.

Grape varieties: cabernet sauvignon (54 percent), merlot (40 percent), cabernet franc (6 percent).

Area: 1,625 acres (1994).

Production: 924,000 gallons on average.

Characteristics: Deeply colored, fruity, full-bodied wines. They often exhibit more robustness but less finesse than neighboring appellations.

Moulis

Even though it includes seven villages, this is the smallest of the Médoc appellations, at only 7.4 miles long and about half a mile wide. The name Moulis (true

connoisseurs pronounce the final "s") is a reminder that there were once windmills (*moulins* in French) in the area. It obtained its *appellation d'origine contrôlée* in 1938. Like its neighbor Listrac, it has a more continental climate than other appellations, with more pronounced risks of frosts. The land is characterized by several gravelly hilltops.

Left out of the classification of 1855, Moulis remained in obscurity for a long time, to the joy of some informed connoisseurs who knew where to find excellent wines at very reasonable prices. Only Chasse-Spleen has been well known for some time, thanks to its romantic name (no one knows whether it was inspired by Baudelaire or Lord Byron), but also because of the quality of its wine, which has been acclaimed by Robert Parker and American buyers. Fairly austere when young, it is a wine that requires many years of aging before it really opens up.

The efforts to improve quality that have been undertaken recently by many estates have paid off, especially when the first vintages of 1990 suffered from very difficult weather conditions, with terrible freezes and heavy rains. Moulis's fame has been increasing, but there are still many fine discoveries to be made by the discerning wine lover.

Poujeaux has become one of the leaders of the appellation thanks to its insistence on high quality. During the 1991 harvest, although only 30 percent of volume survived a frost, the Theil family still eliminated half of it to obtain the desired quality in its wine. The Grands-Poujeaux area is one of the best of the appellation.

The other leader is no doubt Maucaillou, which is lovingly cared for by the Dourthe family, who also manage the Maucaillou estate in Listrac. In addition to making high-quality wines, the château houses a museum devoted to the arts of winegrowing and winemaking that is worth a visit.

IDENTIFICATION

Type: red wine.

Grape varieties: cabernet sauvignon (54 percent), merlot (40 percent), cabernet franc (6 percent).

Area: 1,472 acres (1994).

Production: between 660,000 and 792,000 gallons on average.

Characteristics: Mellow wines with a bouquet characterized by finesse and charm.

Saint-Julien

Because Saint-Julien is located between Margaux and Pauillac, it is often said that its wines have the finesse of one and the body of the other. Some wine experts even claim that the closer a vineyard is situated to the north (near Pauillac) or the south (toward Margaux), the more the wines are like one or the other.

They may be right, as the appellation (which has only one village, Saint-Julien-Beychevelle) is located primarily on two plateaus, one with pebbly and the other with gravelly soil. But the wines still have their own particular style marked by balance and consistency, with a great capacity for aging.

On a relatively small area of land, there are no fewer than eleven *crus classés,* five of them *seconds crus.* Stars are not lacking here, but there are hardly any *crus bourgeois* for the impecunious wine lover to discover.

IDENTIFICATION

Type: red wine.

Grape varieties: cabernet sauvignon (54 percent), merlot (40 percent), cabernet franc (6 percent).

Area: 2,250 acres (1994).

Production: 1.3 million gallons on average.

Characteristics: Well-balanced wines that combine finesse and body, with a great deal of harmony.

• Léoville. Until the French Revolution, this was a single estate named after a noble domain in Charente. The seizure of the goods of émigrés and the denial of birthrights led to the splitting up of the estate into three properties, all of them classified as *seconds crus.*

Léoville-Las-Cases, next to the famed Château Latour, is completely surrounded by walls, and its gate is adorned with a stone lion that has become one of the best-known symbols of the Médoc. Many believe that its equally well-known wine deserves the status of a *premier cru.*

Léoville-Poyferré, the smallest of the three, has been managed for more than seventy years by the Cuvelier family, which also owns Moulin-Riche, one of the rare *crus bourgeois* of Saint-Julien.

The third, Léoville-Barton, is named for the illustrious Irish family that has been

Château Lagrange and its beautiful park.

trading in Bordeaux wines since 1722, the founders of the Barton & Guestier (Seagram group) merchant house. It was Hugh Barton who bought the Léoville estate in 1826, five years after he bought Château Langoa, another Saint-Julien *cru classé.*

The château, a gorgeous manor house, and the winemaking equipment are the same for both vineyards, but the wine production of each is kept completely separate. Anthony Barton, "the most Irish of Médocains," presides over the two estates.

• Beychevelle. This estate boasts one of the most beautiful classic châteaux in the Médoc. Built at the beginning of the eighteenth century, it has a superb view of the Gironde. Its name is a deformation of *baisse voile* (lower sails), as the boats passing the château used to drop their sails to

salute the Duc d'Épernon, grand admiral of France and lord of Beychevelle. Later, Beychevelle, the flagship castle of the Médoc, became the property of a Mr. Conte. Then the château was owned by the Achille-Fould family, which sent many politicians to the French Empire and the Republic. The property now belongs to the insurance company G.M.F.

• Gruaud-Larose. Founded in the eighteenth century by Mr. Gruaud, the vineyard received a hyphenated name when his daughter married Joseph-Sébastien de la Rose, lieutenant-general of Guyenne. The estate was divided in two in the nineteenth century because of an inheritance dispute, but it was considered as a whole for the classification of 1855. It was brought back together in 1934 by Désiré Cordier, a merchant who fled from Lorraine during World War I and set up

With its two large towers, the imposing manor house at Ducru-Beaucaillou looks like a palace amid the vines.

business in the Médoc. Later bought by Pierre Suard for the Alcatel group, this *second cru* offers consistent quality. Today, it belongs to the Bernard Taillan group.

• Ducru-Beaucaillou. Around 1795, Bertrand Ducru, the new owner of the Beaucaillou estate, added his name to it and built a manor house, which is today the main building. An anecdote recounts that nearly a century later, the estate steward made an important discovery. To frighten away grape thieves, he painted the feet of the most-exposed vines blue with a copper sulfate solution. To his great surprise, those vines were not attacked by downy mildew. This mixture of copper sulfate, chalk, and water known as *bouillie bordelaise* was later perfected by the researchers Millardet and Gayon.

Ducru-Beaucaillou has been the property of the Borie family for more than fifty years, and its wines are some of the most perfect expressions of the Saint-Julien style.

• Lagrange. A Tuscan-style tower was added to this charming Louis XVI-style house at the beginning of the nineteenth century. The estate once covered 741 acres, a huge area for the Médoc, but later shrank. Today, it has 277 acres of vines. Poorly managed for a time, it was in very bad shape when it was purchased by the Japanese group Suntory in 1983. This acquisition raised protests, but the Japanese invested heavily and brought Lagrange back to its former splendor.

• Saint-Pierre. This *quatrième cru classé* was divided into two distinct vineyards for some time, which didn't prevent it from being classified as a single entity in 1855. Never very well known, it was rebuilt after its purchase in 1982 by Henri Martin, who also owns Château Gloria, a cru bourgeois in Saint-Julien.

• Talbot. This vineyard carries the name of a fifteenth-century English general. Since 1918, it has belonged to the descendants of Désiré Cordier, once the owner of the famous merchant house Cordier.

• Branaire-Ducru. Once known as Braneyre, this property passed into the hands of Mr. Duluc in 1666, and was later owned by Gustave Ducru. Its official name is Château Branaire (Duluc-Ducru), but it is commonly called Branaire-Ducru. The four crowns on the label are a reminder of illustrious visitors Count Ravez, Count de La Tour, Marquis de Marsac, and Viscount de Larsan.

Pauillac

The best-known of the Bordeaux appellations owes its prestige to the presence of three *premiers crus classés,* superb *crus bourgeois,* and even to its cooperative. The quality of the appellation comes above all from its soil of gravelly hilltops on the two plateaus to the north and south of the small town of Pauillac. They provide deep drainage, forcing the vine's roots to stretch out in search of the moisture necessary for their growth. The vines are very dense and are practically the only crop grown in the area.

The nearby Gironde estuary ensures a mild climate, and, in some places, like Latour, freezes are nearly nonexistent.

The names of some vineyards, like Latour and Lafite, were already known and appreciated by the end of the seventeenth century, and their prestige has continued into the present. Pauillac has always set the tone in the Médoc, and it was here that most of the experiments in winegrowing and winemaking were conducted. These innovations have led to constant improvements in the standards of the Bordeaux region's wines. And, thanks to their high standards, the Pauillac wines have served as ambassadors around the world for other Bordeaux wines.

Aside from the *crus classés,* the surface area covered with vines in Pauillac is extensive (a total of 2,347 acres). This means that many merchants can buy excellent wines to improve the blends that are sold under their own labels.

• Lafite-Rothschild. The name Lafite (sometimes formerly spelled Lafitte or Laffitte) belonged to a lord who lived during the reign of Saint Louis. It comes from an old Gascon word, *hite,* meaning "hillock" or "mound." The first vineyards probably appeared here in the sixteenth century, and their size doubled between 1670 and 1784, when the property belonged to the de Ségur family. Nicknamed the "Prince of Vines," Nicolas-Alexandre de Ségur owned not only Lafite but also Latour, Mouton, and what would later become Calon-Ségur. At the time of the French Revolution, the estate was seized as national property and was then sold at auction. Although it later changed hands frequently, it was managed for a long time by the same steward, a Mr. Goudal.

On August 8, 1868, Lafite was bought by James de Rothschild for the (at the time) outrageous sum of 4.44 million French francs. The story goes that the baron, who wanted to buy a Médoc property, as other Parisian bankers had done, chose Lafite because his bank's headquarters were located on Rue Laffitte in Paris. But it was also "the best vineyard in the Médoc, producing the best wine in Bordeaux," according to a poster advertising its sale at auction in 1797. James de Rothschild himself never set foot on the estate, which remained the property of the Rothschild bank and its successive barons.

On its 222 acres of vines are planted cabernet sauvignon (seventy percent), merlot (twenty percent), and cabernet franc (ten percent), with an average production of 350,000 bottles, including a second wine, Moulin-de-Carruades, which is one of the oldest of its type. The wines of Lafite-Rothschild render some wine critics grandiloquent. In "Le Classement de 1996" *(Revue de Vin de France,* Flammarion), Michel Bettane wrote: "The magnificent sand and gravel soil on a limestone base provides the cabernet sauvignon with an unequaled tannic delicacy, while human expertise has perfected an original style of light, spicy wine, with the compelling and unique aromas of almonds and violets. It has a texture of transcendental finesse."

• Latour. The name and the image used on the label refer to the turbulent history

IDENTIFICATION

Type: red wine.

Grape varieties: cabernet sauvignon (54 percent), Merlot (40 percent), cabernet franc (6 percent).

Area: 2,895 acres (1994).

Production: 1.6 million gallons on average.

Characteristics: Well-bred wines, opulent and full-bodied, but with a great deal of elegance. Often austere when young, they blossom after years of aging and retain a remarkable balance.

of the region during the middle ages. Originally, this estate was a fortified town exposed to attacks by pirates and the opponents in the wars between the French and the English for the possession of Guyenne. The vineyard began to draw attention at the end of the seventeenth century, when it became part of the holdings of the de Ségur family, along with Lafite and later Mouton and Calon. It was separated from Lafite in 1760, and, despite some ups and downs, succeeded in maintaining its integrity and improving the quality of its wines. For generations, the Ségur family owned all or at least a majority of the company set up in 1842. This continued until the arrival of the British groups Pearson and Bristol in 1962.

The tower that stands on the estate is not original. It dates to the eighteenth century, while the château itself was built during the Second Empire. For a long time there was no house at all on the property.

The current vineyard has an area of 148 acres, 116 of them reserved for first wines and the rest used for the making of Forts-de-Latour. Total production is around 200,000 bottles. Cabernet sauvignon is by far the predominant variety, taking up eighty percent of the vineyard, with fifteen percent for merlot and five percent for cabernet franc and petit-verdot.

Its microclimate protects Latour from nearly all risk of frost, an important advantage. The soil, made up of large-sized gravel and sand, provides perfect drainage, while the underlayer of clay holds the necessary moisture during the summer. These conditions doubtlessly explain why Latour is one of the most consistent wines of Pauillac, with very few vintages that are not completely up to the standards of the estate.

In the 1994 edition of his *Guide to the Wines of France,* Robert Parker describes the 1990 Latour as the most refined and typical of the Latours, with a colorful, opaque personality that is strong and powerful, marking the return to the great qualities that have made this estate famous throughout most of this century. He finds the bouquet still closed but promising the aromas of minerals, grilled walnuts, and perfumed, perfectly ripe black currants. In the mouth, he finds it powerful, with a massive intensity, overflowing with fat, very rich in extracts and in aggressive tannins. "It literally explodes in the mouth," he says.

• Pichon-Longueville. Two châteaux carry this name and, while they are neighbors, there is little resemblance when it comes to the quality of their wines, both

Bottles being labeled and sealed at Château Latour, where the labels are still glued on by hand. The bottles are wrapped in tissue paper and packed in wooden cases stamped with the chateau's name.

of them classified as *seconds crus*. They both spring from the same estate, dating to the seventeenth century, that bore the name of Jacques de Pichon, baron of Longueville, in the eighteenth century. One of his descendants divided the estate in two, one for his sons (Pichon-Longueville) and the other for his daughters (Pichon-Longueville-Comtesse-de-Lalande). They were at first managed as a single unit, but eventually became independent. Pichon-Longueville (commonly referred to in Bordeaux as Pichon-Baron) was the property of the Bouteiller family for a long time, before being purchased in 1987 by the Axa group. Planted mostly with cabernet sauvignon (seventy-five percent), the 123-acre estate produces excellent wines that sometimes approach the level of quality of the neighboring Lafite estate thanks to their amazing complexity. The château (1851), with slender turrets and colonnades, is one of the most graceful in the Médoc.

Pichon-Longueville-Comtesse-de-Lalande became the property of Édouard Miailhe in 1925, and his daughter, Madame de Lencquesaing, has been managing it since 1978. The traditional mix of grape varieties is better respected on this 177.8 acre vineyard, with fifty-seven percent cabernet sauvignon, thirty-five percent merlot, and eight percent petit-verdot. The resulting wines are charming and fruity, with strong tannins but plenty of silky notes.

• Duhart-Milon-Rothschild. Located next to Château Lafite,. this estate belonged for many years to the Castéja family.

They owned it when its wines were ranked as the only *quatrième cru* in Pauillac in the 1855 classification. In 1962, Duhart-Milon was purchased by its powerful neighbor, who added the Rothschild name to the estate. The estates were managed by the same people, but they respected the differences between the two vineyards. Cabernet sauvignon accounts for sixty-five percent of the mix, along with merlot (twenty-eight percent) and cabernet franc (seven percent), on a 148-acre vineyard.

• Pontet-Canet. In 1750, a Mr. de Pontet bought this property located in Canet, near Mouton, and added his name to the estate's. The Cruse family later owned it for more than a century, expanding both the vineyard and the château. The equipment was modernized regularly, especially under the steward named Skavinsky, who also took care of several other Médoc *crus classés*. In 1975, Guy Tesseron, a native of Charente and already the owner of another *cru classé,* bought the

estate. His first decision was to bottle his wines at the château, as Pontet-Canet was one of the last *crus classés* that wasn't estate-bottled. This superb 296-acre estate (including 193 acres of vines, most of them cabernet sauvignon) has improved greatly in quality, thanks to the advice of

the oenologist Émile Peynaud. It now produces wines that are a perfect expression of the Pauillac style.

- Grand-Puy-Ducasse and Grand-Puy-Lacoste. These two vineyards, located on the Bages plateau, must have originally belonged to the same estate. Lacoste (also called Saint-Guirons, after a former owner) has the eighteenth-century château. The estate was purchased in 1932 by Raymond Dupin, who had no children and sought a winegrower capable of even-

WINE LABELS

These two labels date from different eras. The one on top is from the 1930s, the other is recent. The first describes the wine as a *grand cru*

classé du Haut Médoc—not allowed today. This was meant to designate wines as being from upper (*haut*) or lower (*bas*) Médoc, before the Pauillac appellation was created. This label represents an intermediate stage between the time when all wines produced in the the region were identified simply as "Bordeaux" and the present practice of identifying the local appellation.
The older label also carries the boastful description—*Grands Vins de Pauillac, les premiers vins du monde*—"The Great Wines of Pauillac, the best wines in the world!"

tually taking over. He found the right person in Eugène Borie, already the owner of Ducru-Beaucaillou, who inherited Dupin's estate in 1980. Under his management, the vineyard produces a purebred Pauillac.

The situation of Grand-Puy-Ducasse is more complicated. Parcels of separate vineyards surround the Lacoste estate, but the château and the winemaking installations are located in Pauillac on the banks of the Gironde. Not very well known in the past, the vineyard has been reinvigorated over the past few years.

- Lynch-Bages. Located to the south of Pauillac, the Bages plateau has lent its name to several vineyards, with the addition of the names of the families that owned them. Lynch-Bages is the best known of them. Its wines have an unusually strong style that is spicy, with balsamic notes and an astonishing mellowness. It is so highly admired that it sells for the price of a *second cru*. Its name comes from an Irish Catholic family that came to Bordeaux in the seventeenth century. Since 1934, the Cazes family has restored the estate to its former glory. A half-bottle of 1975 Lynch-Bages had the honor of being the first bottle of Bordeaux to orbit the earth—114 times—when it was taken on the space shuttle Discovery in 1985 by the French astronaut Patrick Baudry.
- Lynch-Moussas. This estate has belonged to the Castéja family, one of the old families of the region, since 1919.

Their name appears in records dating as far back as the thirteenth century, and they have served as notaries, landowners, and merchants. It is said that Lynch-Moussas was long a favorite hunting spot and that it was not unusual to see Alfonso XIII, king of Spain, there. The Castéjas also own the neighboring Batailley vineyard, and they have undertaken a major renovation of this long-neglected estate.

- Haut-Bages-Libéral is also broken up into separate parcels. One attractive vineyard is near Château Latour, and others are on the Bages plateau. Recently taken over by the team that rejuvenated Chasse-Spleen (Bernadette Villars and her daughter, Claire), the vineyard should soon be worthy once again of its former reputation.
- Croizet-Bages belonged to the Calvé family for many years, and its château is separate from the vineyard. Since 1934, it has been the property of the Quié family, Bordeaux merchants.
- Batailley. The name refers to a decisive battle (*bataille*, in French), in which the French beat the English during the Hundred Years' War. The estate once

belonged to Mr. Guestier (of the trading company Barton & Guestier) and later to the Borie family, owners of another trading company, which still handles distribution for the current owners, the Castéja family. The well-known Batailley contributed a great deal to the popularity of the wines of Pauillac. Its neighbor, Haut-Batailley, has been reunited with it after having been shared with another branch of the Borie family. There is no château, but there is an unusual tower topped with a statue of the Virgin Mary, erected by a pious woman who hoped it would protect the vineyard from phylloxera.

- Armailhac. In the eighteenth century, this estate was part of Mouton, which belonged to the Brane family. It was divided in 1853, with one part becoming Mouton-Rothschild and the other being bought by an agronomist named d'Armailhacq. In 1933, Philippe de Rothschild bought the estate, and its name then changed several times, becoming successively Mouton d'Armailhac, Mou-

ton-Baron-Philippe, Mouton-Baronne-Philippe (in honor of Baron Philippe's second wife, the American Pauline Fairfax Potter), and, most recently, Armailhac. Through all these name changes, the wine has continued to be well made and consistent.

• Clerc-Millon.This small estate, with fifty-nine acres of vines, is located near Mouton and Lafite. It produces a Pauillac with great character, complexity and persistence, making it worthy of its great neighbors. In 1970, it became the property of Philippe de Rothschild.

• Pédesclaux. This estate was created in the early nineteenth century by the unification of several parcels of land detached from the Grand-Puy estate. The Jugla family ran it as tenant farmers from 1931 to 1950 when they bought the estate.

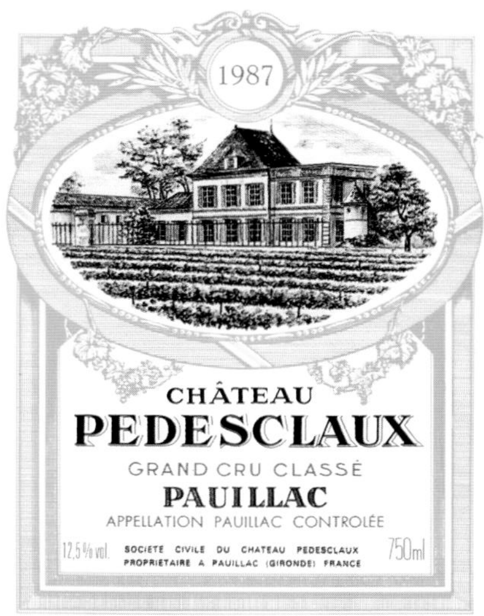

Apart from the *crus classés,* the following châteaux are also worthy of interest. Bernadotte *(cru bourgeois)* is a reminder of the kings of Sweden and their interests in Bordeaux. In good years, Fonbadet is a *cru bourgeois* in the best Pauillac style. Pibran is a *cru bourgeois* that belongs to the insurance company Axa and is well run by the Cazes family of Lynch-Bages. La Bécasse, as its name would indicate (it means "woodcock" in French), does indeed go well with game. La Rose Pauillac is a highly honorable wine produced by the local cooperative.

WINE LABELS

Until the beginning of the twentieth century, wine, even a *cru classé,* was always sold in barrels to a merchant, who was responsible for the aging and bottling. The merchants then put their own labels on the bottles. The identical vintage from the same château could therefore wind up in bottles with completely different labels, depending on which merchant purchased the original wine.

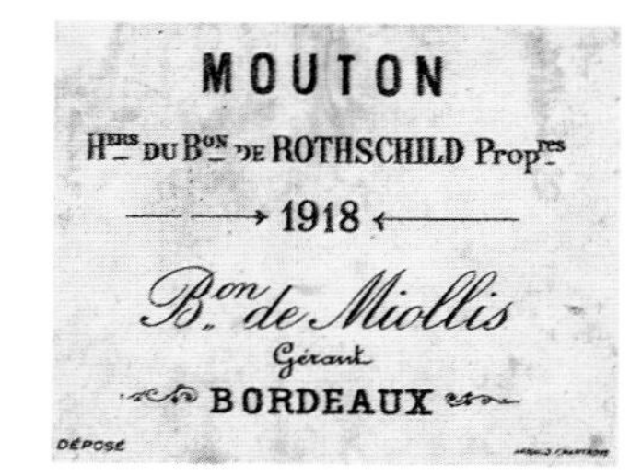

The label on the left dates from before the purchase of Mouton by Nathaniel de Rothschild, when the vineyard was still known as Brane-Mouton.

In 1924, Philippe de Rothschild made a decision that was revolutionary at the time: he would bottle his own wine at the château. This was an important change because it meant that the estate owner became totally responsible for his wine, which hadn't been the case before. To celebrate the event, Philippe de Rothschild asked the famous poster designer Jean Carlu to create an original label for him (the bottle on the left below). This innovation, along with the fact that Jean Carlu was known for his advertising work (some of it was wonderful, but it was still advertising) caused a stir in the Médoc.The story doesn't end there, however. At the end of World War II, Baron Philippe had the idea of dedicating the 1945 vintage to the end of the war. He asked the young painter Philippe Jullian for a graphic composition featuring a "V" for "victory." This one-time event ended up becoming a tradition and, since 1946, a different contemporary artist has been asked to create an original work to illustrate the Mouton label each year. The resulting works form a remarkable gallery of modern art, with works by Jean Cocteau, Léonor Fini, Jean Hugo, Marie Laurencin, Carzou, Georges Braque, Masson, Dalí, Mathieu, Miró, Chagall, Paul Delvaux, César, Agam, Keith Haring, and even Picasso (bottle in center below; work reprinted with the permission of Paloma Picasso), who designed the label for the 1973 bottle, and Francis Bacon, for the 1990 label.

This snuffbox dating to the 1830s is decorated with a ram's head, the symbol of the Scottish regiments. It was a gift to Baron Philippe de Rothschild.

MOUTON-ROTHSCHILD

In spite of the collection of ram heads and other representations of the sheep family found in the various rooms of the estate, the name Mouton ("sheep" in French) has nothing to do with the woolly animal. It is derived from the Old French word *mothon,* which means "small hill."

The estate has a long aristocratic history: it was successively owned by the Duke of Gloucester, Gaston de Foix, the Duc d'Épernon, and, finally, the Baron de Brane. In 1853, it was bought by Nathaniel de Rothschild, who gave it his name. The estate has belonged to his descendants ever since.

For more than a century, the vineyard was the victim of an injustice: it was not given top ranking in the 1855 classification and was instead placed among the second wines. The decision had been far from unanimous, however. In 1867, Alfred Danflou noted that "at the London Exposition in 1862, Mouton was ranked almost at the level of the *grands crus,* and it deserved to be completely assimilated. The time has come to award it its place among royalty. Public opinion agrees, and, in this case, public opinion should have the force of law."

One man was responsible for the elevation of Mouton to the top ranking: Philippe de Rothschild, the great-grandson of Nathaniel. He took over the estate in 1922, at a time when a serious crisis had hit the Bordeaux region. Ahead of his time in every sense, he restored the equipment and pioneered estate-bottling as early as 1924. At a time when no outsiders ever visited the estates, he built a superb *chai* that was open to the public and later added a wine museum that now also houses works of art, with everything from ancient Egyptian works to Picassos. There is nothing else like it in the world.

In 1945, he had another innovative idea. For the label of each new vintage, he asked one of the most famous painters of the day to come up with an illustration. Cocteau, Dalí, Mathieu, César, Chagall, Picasso, Delvaux, and Warhol all responded, creating a collection that is almost as valuable as the wine itself (see box on page 69). In addition, each label bore the signature of Philippe de Rothschild and the number of bottles, including magnums and jeroboams, in the vintage. The label on the 1993 vintage, by the painter Balthus, represents a nude woman and caused a furor in America, creating great publicity for the wine.

Baron Philippe de Rothschild fought for decades to have Mouton classified in the top rankings. He finally won the battle in 1973. To this day, it is the only time that the 1855 classification has been changed.

His daughter, Philippine de Rothschild, continues the work of her father, who died in 1988. While maintaining the quality of Mouton, she continues to expand the activities of the trading company, long called La Baronnie and now named Philippe de Rothschild S.A. Located in Pauillac, the company has a star in its Mouton-Cadet, a Bordeaux *de marque* that has benefited from the fame of the *cru classé,* as well as other satellite labels that are marketed with great success. She regularly crosses the Atlantic to strengthen ties with the best California winegrowers, and she participated in the creation of Opus One, a Pauillac-style American wine made by Robert Mondavi.

The museum at Mouton, organized around one large room and six smaller ones, brings together a magnificent collection of artworks. Works of art also adorn the work areas, the **chais,** *and the park.*

The current vineyard's 178 acres are planted mostly with cabernet sauvignon (eighty-five percent), with some cabernet franc (ten percent) and merlot (five percent). Average annual production is around 300,000 bottles. There is no second wine at Mouton since the wines that are not used for the *premier cru* go into the making of the trading house's generic wines. At once full-bodied and voluptuous, Mouton-Rothschild has great strength as well as finesse and unequaled mellowness. Once known for its note of black currant, the bouquet is becoming more complex, but still has slightly burnt aromas.

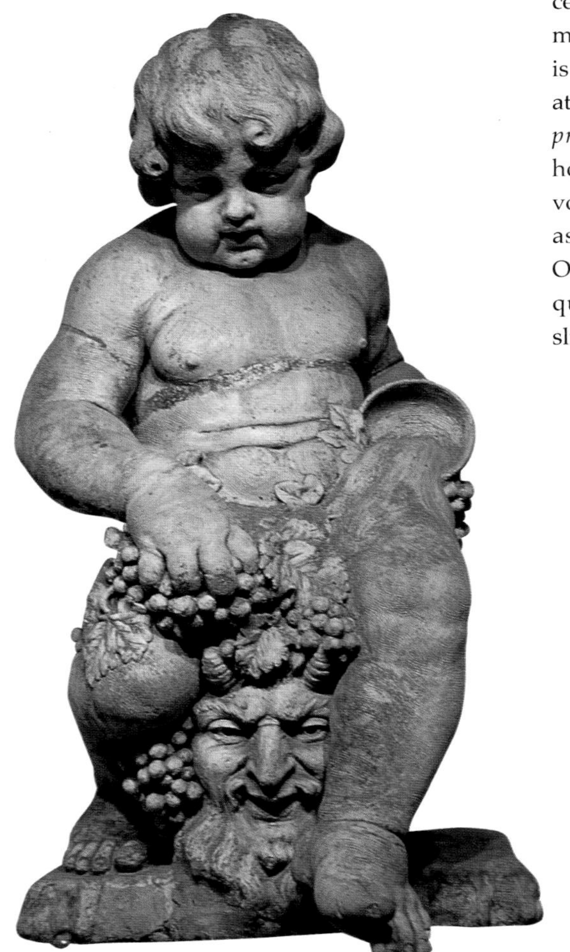

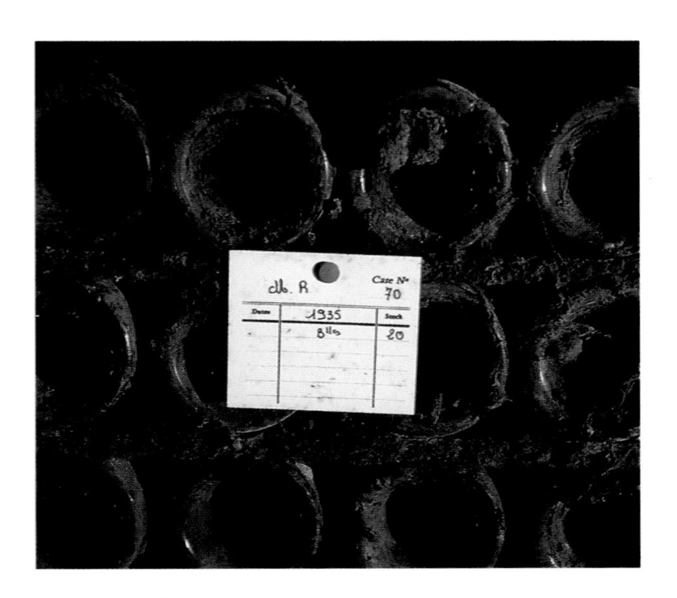

Saint-Estèphe

The most northerly of the Haut Médoc appellations, Saint-Estèphe is very different from the others, and especially from its neighbor Pauillac. With the exception of several acres located in the Pauillac appellation, the Saint-Estèphe vineyards are in the commune of that name.

The characteristics of the wines are due primarily to the soil, made up of sand and gravel, with a higher clay content than elsewhere. The slightly higher proportion of merlot grapes used also sets these wines apart from others. Particularly when young, Saint-Estèphe wines are quite closed up and austere, with little bouquet—although, over the past few years, there has been a trend toward fruitier wines. It must be said that Saint-Estèphe wines are at first taste the least pleasing of the Médoc wines and can be rather disconcerting. In the end, however, they open up and offer great aromatic qualities; as they soften, they release their charm. Many connoisseurs of Médoc wines end up choosing Saint-Estèphe as their favorite.

IDENTIFICATION

Type: red wine.
Grape varieties: cabernet sauvignon (54 percent), merlot (40 percent), cabernet franc (6 percent).
Area: 3,404 acres (1994).
Production: 1.9 million gallons on average.
Characteristics: Powerful, full-bodied wine, high in tannin with a bouquet that is slow to open. Long aging capacity.

The appellation includes five *crus classés,* as well as excellent *crus bourgeois* that deserved a place in the 1855 classification.

• Cos d'Estournel *(second cru classé).* The star of the appellation has a highly unusual château, with a Chinese-style tower and a wine-shed door that comes from the sultanate of Zanzibar. Louis-Gaspard d'Estournel, who had the château built at the beginning of the nineteenth century, did not intend to live in it but wanted to provide the best possible home for his wines. This eccentric character loved horses and boats as much as wine, and he was known to trade barrels of wine for Arab stallions from the Emirates. The story goes that one time there weren't enough horses to fill his order, and he had to have some of his wine sent back to Bordeaux. When it arrived, he tasted it and found that it had improved considerably during the trip. He then decided that all his wine should be sent to Arabia and back before it was drunk! When financial

There is something ceremonious about a visit to the Château Cos d'Estournel, a veritable palace dedicated to wine. The château's interior is as extraordinary as its exterior architecture.

ruin came, he was forced to sell Cos d'Estournel in 1853 to an English banker, Charles Cecil Martyns, who advanced the reputation of the wine and the appellation in general among London high society. In 1917, the vineyard became the property of Fernand Ginestet, who had coveted it for a many years. One of his descendants, Bruno Prats, still owns it and produces fine wine. Cos d'Estournel contains much more merlot than its neighbor, the Lafite cru, and exhibits a unique roundness and body. Bruno Prats also produces Château-Marbuzet wine, on whose estate he makes his home. The wine is a marvel of elegance, and while it is powerfully structured, it has a smooth finish. This is the one to recommend to someone who has difficulty appreciating this appellation.

• Montrose *(second cru classé)*. This fairly recent estate was cleared at the beginning of the nineteenth century by Théodore Dumoulin and didn't reach cruising speed until just before the 1855 classification, in which it managed to reach the second level. The château and outbuildings were constructed by Mathieu Dollfus, the estate's second owner, at the end of the nineteenth century. Montrose then passed into the hands of the Charmolüe family from Compiègne, which has managed to hold on to it, despite some difficulties. They have made it into one of the most handsome estates in the appellation, with 168 uninterrupted acres of vines. Fairly hard when young, these wines require long aging before they reveal their splendor. The estate's second wine, with the charming name, Dame de Montrose, is more modest but can be drunk younger.

• Calon-Ségur *(troisième cru classé)*. This is one of the oldest estates in the appellation, dating to at least the seventeenth century. It is still marked by the personality of Nicolas-Alexandre de Ségur, the "Prince of Wines," who once said: "I make wine at Latour and at Lafite, but my heart is at Calon," which explains the drawing of a heart on the wine's label. At the beginning of the twentieth century, this vineyard was the glory of the appellation, but has since disappointed wine experts because of its inconsistency. If you are visiting Saint-Estèphe, the rather severe Château Calon is worth a detour; with its two square towers, it has its own bourgeois charm.

• Lafon-Rochet *(quatrième cru classé)*. This estate existed as early as 1650, when it was called Rochette. Later, it became very well known, and, although located near Lafite and Cos d'Estournel, the high quality of its wine was recognized by the 1855 classification. Later, the vineyard declined, and it was bought by Guy Tes-

WINE LABELS

One hundred years and a series of new regulations separate these two labels. On the one on the left, the Saint-Estèphe appellation is not mentioned—it did not officially exist until 1936. The wine is described simply as "Médoc."

In addition, there is no reference to the fact that the château has a ranking in the 1855 classification. Today, even though it is not required by the rules, no estate owner would ever neglect to mention this ranking on the label.

The old label does say that it was bottled on the estate, however. This was often added later by the printer at the request of the owner when he bottled part of his wine on the estate. It must not be forgotten that while this seems natural to us today and is even required for *appellation d'origine contrôlée* wines, it was not a universal practice until 1969.

seron in 1959. He had to start practically from scratch, planting new vines and rebuilding the château and other structures. The renovated château is a good example of an eighteenth-century Bordeaux manor house, but only the chapel actually dates to that period. After this complete reconstruction, it took time before the vineyard could once again produce high-quality wines, but this has been accomplished, and the wine now offers an excellent value for its price.

- Cos-Labory *(cinquième cru classé)*. The word *cos* is the local variant on the Gascon term *caux,* which means "hill of pebbles." Detached in 1810 from its neighbor, Cos d'Estournel, the estate was owned for some time by the English banker Martyns. Then Cos-Labory fell into a long slumber before being revitalized by the Audoy family beginning in 1959. This small forty-five acre estate produces wine of great richness that is getting better every year.

- Haut-Marbuzet. For twenty years, the Duboscq family has been making what could be a *grand cru bourgeois* in the Médoc, as it is often superior to the *crus classés.* Made in the traditional way (with heated barrels), the wine is round, even voluptuous, thanks to its high merlot content. As with the other wines of the Saint-Estèphe appellation, one must take one's time to learn to appreciate Haut-Marbuzet wine, but one's patience will be rewarded. The Duboscq family also owns the Chambert-Marbuzet vineyard, which, even though it shares half the name, is not the second wine of Haut-Marbuzet.

- Le Crock. Owned by the Cuvelier family (also the owners of Léoville-Poyferré in Saint-Julien), this *cru bourgeois* has excellent potential. At first taste, the wine surprises by its extremely subtle bouquet, but its structure is revealed at the finish with great finesse.

- Phélan-Ségur. Another high-class *cru bourgeois,* with finesse and opulence and

true aromatic complexity. The Gardiniers, who bought the estate in 1985 after selling the Pommery and Lanson Champagne houses, are raising the value of their wine, which ages very well, every year. The same château produces another interesting wine, Frank Phélan, named after

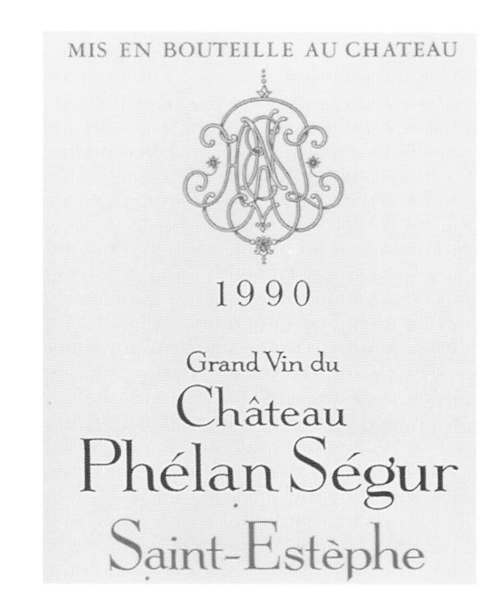

the first owner of the Phélan-Ségur château. This Irishman fell in love with Saint-Estèphe and founded the estate in the nineteenth century. He served as the town's mayor for thirty years.

• De Pez. This excellent *cru bourgeois* is proof that in Saint-Estèphe it is not only *crus classés* that produce supple, full-bodied wines. Thanks to exclusive distribution by the company Gilbey's, the wine is better known in London than in Paris.

Not to be forgotten is Meyney, owned by the Cordier company, which makes a harmonious wine that is as charming as the château itself. Other Saint-Estèphe wines that have a following are Les Ormes de Pez, Tour de Pez, Pomys, Ségur de Cabanac, and Tronquoy-Lalande.

Château Phélan-Ségur.

SECOND WINES

Estates have been marketing second wines under different labels from those of their *crus* since the end of the nineteenth century, but the practice didn't become widespread until after World War II when estate-bottling began to become common. A considerable increase in the number of second wines occurred about thirty years ago.

Second wines are peculiar to the Bordeaux region and are more common in the Médoc than in other areas. They are particularly appropriate to the way wines are produced in the Médoc because the estates there are fairly large, of at least several dozen acres. On such large areas, some parcels of land, even within the same vineyard, are bound to have some differences in their soil, exposure to the sun, and the age of the vines.

Bordeaux wine is essentially a blend, and the art of the winemaker consists of composing his final wine by bringing together different products, that is, the different grape varieties. When the first barrel aging is finished, the tasting begins. This is where the mixing comes in; the idea is to obtain the best possible wine, with a unique style. During this period, the tasters decide on a selection, with a first, second, and even a third choice.

The second wine of some famous *crus* brings together wines of true quality, and, rather than produce them outside of the classification, they are sold under another label, which at least indicates their connection to a prestigious château. The commercial success of second wines did not occur until the practice became more common. In this way, wine lovers are able to buy quality bottles at less-astronomical prices than those of some *crus*. Buying a Les-Carruades-de-Lafite, a Forts-de-Latour, or a Margaux Pavillon-Rouge is something of a thrill in itself, bringing the buyer closer to the stars of the Médoc.

It is true that second wines never achieve the opulence or complexity of *premiers crus,* but they provide a good idea of what the top wines are like. For beginners, they are also a good introduction to the great wines.

When dreaming up names for their second wines that refer to the name of the château, some owners have indulged a bit too much in fantasy, using names of châteaux that never existed. Others have used names that have absolutely nothing to do with that of the first wine, hoping to give the second wine an independent life.

The phenomenon has grown so much that we are even beginning to see the appearance of third wines, such as at Léoville-Las-Cases, made from wine considered not good enough for the second wine! Happily, this practice is still very limited.

Second wines are often disparaged by wine experts who feel that the prices charged by the

owners have more to do with the fame of the first wine than with the intrinsic quality of the wine being sold. Robert Parker, the well-known American wine critic, rates as "pleasant," "very good," or "excellent" only one-quarter of the 120 second wines he has tasted. He rates the others as of "average quality" or "without interest."

While we do not necessarily agree with his point of view, it must be admitted that this practice has the downside of increasing the number of labels in the Bordeaux region, making it even more difficult for amateur wine lovers, especially outside France, to find wines they like. It may even turn them away from vineyards that seem impenetrable. But, for those who are willing to go to the trouble, there are some fine discoveries to be made among the second wines, especially in the great years, when their qualities are best revealed. And, in any case, these are mostly wines that are very well made, benefiting as they do from the same expertise as the first wines since the selection is made only after the final blending.

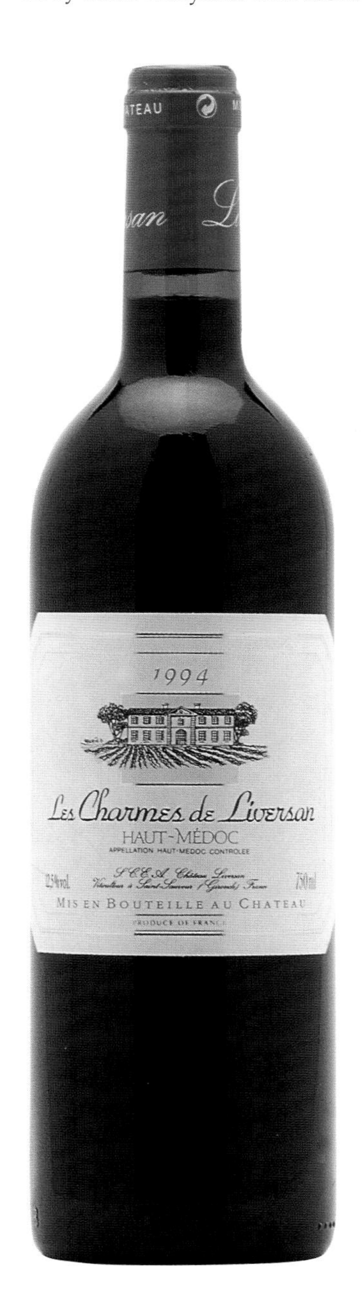

GRAVES

The Graves district stretches from the suburbs of Bordeaux to Sauternes along the left bank of the Garonne River. Vines have been cultivated here since the Roman era, making it the oldest winegrowing area in the Bordeaux region. Its name comes literally from the earth, from the gravelly, sandy soil (*graves* in French) that is so well-suited to the production of quality wines. The first "clarets," which made the reputation of Bordeaux wine in the British market and formed the basis of the prosperity of the city's middle classes and merchants, were produced here.

Great red wines are made in Graves, including those of Haut-Brion (the only wine from outside the Médoc that was listed in the classification of 1855), along with the best whites made in Bordeaux. The revolution in white wine began in Graves, where new vinification techniques were first introduced.

The Graves district suffered in the nineteenth century as the growing city of Bordeaux ate away at its land and phylloxera ate away at its vines. The area lost ground to other Bordeaux winegrowing areas and didn't come fully back to life until after World War II, with the establishment in 1959 of a classification of the best vineyards. In 1987, the Pessac-Léognan appellation was created, increasing the value of the best wines. Since then, a new generation of winegrowers has thrown itself with passion into the improvement of the vineyards and the quality of the wine.

Left: The wine-stained barrels of the first-year wines in Fieuzal's chai.
Above: Château Haut-Bergey in Léognan.

Graves

The long history of Graves has not been tranquil, linked as it was to that of Bordeaux and Aquitaine. The city of Burdigala was founded by the Bituriges

IDENTIFICATION

Type: red and white wines.

Grape varieties: Reds: cabernet sauvignon (39 percent), merlot (48 percent), cabernet franc (13 percent). Whites: sémillon (73 percent), sauvignon (21 percent), muscadelle (6 percent).

Area: Reds: 5,143 acres. Whites: 2,529 acres. (1994).

Production: Reds: 2.5 million gallons on average. Whites: 1.1 million gallons on average.

Characteristics: The elegant, fruity, full-bodied reds are distinguished by an unusual bouquet. The whites are full-bodied and aromatic, with plenty of fat and aromatic finesse.

Vivisques, a Gallic people who had been chased out of Berry by Vercingetorix. They gave their name to *Vitis biturica,* the vine that is the ancestor of cabernet sauvignon. As elsewhere in Gaul, the Roman occupation led to the development of the region's vineyards, which were later mostly destroyed during the Viking and Saracen invasions.

The revitalization of Graves took place in the middle ages. Vines were cultivated near the city of Bordeaux by bishops, nobles, and the middle classes. What are now suburbs were still rural areas at the time, and the gravelly soil was particularly suitable to the production of quality wines. The hilltops of the surrounding parishes were cleared for the production of claret, which was both consumed locally and exported, with the trade monopolized by the middle classes.

In 1152, the marriage of Eleanor of Aquitaine to Henry Plantagenet, future king of England, united the province with Britain for the following two centuries, opening the door for Graves wines not only to the English market, but also to that of northern Europe. This "city wine," as Graves was called at the time, took precedence over other wines, and it was only when there were shortages that the Bordeaux traders allowed the export of wines from the "high country" (Saint-Macaire on the Garonne and Sainte-Foy-La-Grande on the Dordogne).

Even when Aquitaine returned to French hands in the fifteenth century, the expansion of the Graves vineyards continued toward the south along the Garonne as far as Martillac and Labrède. Their

growth led some people to call for limits on the vineyards or even for the elimination of some of them. The Bordeaux bourgeoisie didn't take this lying down, however. Their spokesman, Montesquieu, who himself owned a vineyard in Martillac, said: "If we eliminate vines in Guienne, other parts of France and other countries will increase theirs, and we will be the losers. The uncultivated areas of Guienne include land that is suited for producing the most excellent wines, and the planting of vines should be encouraged, not discouraged".

Graves slowly declined after the French Revolution and during the nineteenth century. The vineyards themselves were under siege, and the English market was closed for several years because of the blokades imposed during the Napoleonic wars, causing the Bordeaux bourgeoisie to

The* graves*, the famous mixture of sand and pebbles that gave its name to the appellation. The soil and climate of Graves are the envy of winegrowers around the world.

THE CLASSIFICATION OF GRAVES VINEYARDS

This classification was established between 1953 and 1959. It does not rate the quality of the wines, but does distinguish between red and white wines. Its main value was as a confirmation of the best vineyards of the time, all of which can now be found in the Pessac-Léognan appellation. It has never been revised and does not take into account the great changes that have occurred since it was established.

- Bouscaut: red and white
- Carbonnieux: red and white
- Couhins: white
- Couhins-Lurton: white
- Domaine de Chevalier: red and white
- Fieuzal: red
- Haut-Bailly: red
- Haut-Brion: red
- Latour-Haut-Brion: red
- La Tour-Martillac: red and white
- Laville-Haut-Brion: white
- La Mission Haut-Brion: red
- Malartic-Lagravière: red and white
- Olivier: red and white
- Pape-Clément: red
- Smith-Haut-Lafitte: red

lose interest in their wines and allowing the Médoc to prosper.

A virulent attack of downy mildew in 1851 partly explains why only one of the Graves estates, Haut-Brion, was included in the classification of 1855. Phylloxera followed in 1863, then the twentieth century brought two world wars. At the same time, Bordeaux's urban sprawl continued to eat away at the region, accounting for the disappearance of four-fifths of the Graves vineyards—more than seven thousand acres of vines and several hundred vineyards—between the beginning of the century and the 1970s.

The resuscitation of the Graves vineyards occurred in various stages. In 1950, the appellation's association, aware that the survival of Graves depended on it, officially requested the Institut national des appellations d'origine to classify its vineyards. They attached to their request a list of 114 estates. A committee of wine brokers was formed, but it came up with a severe verdict: only fifteen red and five white crus were included in a non-hierarchical classification. Its choices were justified by "the fame of a vineyard and the quality of its wines." The association members were furious and refused to accept the decision, but there was nothing to be done. The classification was ratified by decree on August 7, 1953. This provoked more protests, but a second decree, dated February 16, 1959, approved the classification that is still in force today, with thirteen red and nine white *crus*. Some estates were ranked only for the one color that made up most of their produc-

tion at the time, but the situation might be different today.

In 1987, the Pessac-Léognan *appellation d'origine contrôlée* was created. Located in the north sections of the Graves region (see following pages), the appellation proved to be a boon for the whole district because it contained all the *crus classés* of Graves.

Over the past twenty years, dynamic winegrowers have been revitalizing the Graves vineyards with a systematic replanting program: 1,112 acres have been reclaimed over the past fifteen years, and the goal is to increase the surface area to what it was in the 1930s by the year 2000. The current Graves appellation extends from Labrède and Beautiran to Mazères and Saint-Pardon-de-Conques in the south, with the notable exception of the sweet wines of Cérons, Barsac, and Sauternes. The soil is made up of

deposits of gravel and pebbles left behind by the Garonne over the centuries.

Graves is unique in that most of its estates produce both red wine and dry white wine, with some highly successful results for the latter. With the help of the Institut d'œnologie de Bordeaux, the whites have improved appreciably in quality over the past twenty years and have cleaner, fuller aromas, often with a great deal of body and a complex structure. Barrel-aging and more attentive care at every stage of the vinification process can be credited for these changes.

The appellation is still heterogeneous and has fewer standouts than the Pessac-Léognan *crus* (whether or not they are classified), but there are a few vineyards that deserve special attention: Archambeau, for its dry white wines that age well; Ardennes, with well-balanced wines that are representative of the appellation; Brondelle, near Langon, with its fruity whites; Camus for its flowery white that is smooth and lengthy; Chantegrive, with interesting, fruity reds and distinguished whites; Clos Floridène, where Denis Dubourdieu, one of the great oenologists of Bordeaux, puts his expertise into practice; Grand Bos, where the restoration of the eighteenth-century manor house has accompanied the improving quality of the wines; Magneau, with reds and whites that make the best of a remarkable soil; Rahoul, where only sémillon is used for the whites, which have an amazing aging capacity; Seuil, a renovated vineyard that produces a fine white; Vieux Château Gaubert, which makes fine whites and

WINE LABELS

Before Pessac-Léognan became a separate *appellation d'origine contrôlée* in 1987, the vineyards that now claim the appellation were allowed to add to their labels, in addition to the mention of Graves, the denomination Graves Léognan or Graves Pessac, according to their location, in order to distinguish themselves from other Graves vineyards. This 1983 Château Bouscaut label is one such example.

reds, and has a beautiful eighteenth-century château that has escaped the ravages of real estate speculation.

Graves Supérieurs

Graves Supérieurs can be made anywhere in the Graves appellation. They are sweet *(liquoreux)* wines with a small production that has nevertheless been growing over the past few years. They are often made on estates near the more famous names of Sauternes or Barsac. To complicate the matter, wines of the Cérons appellation, which is surrounded by Graves, can also be classified as Graves Supérieurs.

Production techniques are similar to those used for other *liquoreux* white wines, but the results are different because the vines are grown in different soil.

Interestingly, the Dutch market has always been fond of Graves Supérieurs, but, in general, this appellation is not well known, depriving producers of the motivation to make the necessary efforts to achieve the best possible results. There is one exception, however: the Graves Supérieur made by Vins et Domaines H. de Montesquieu. Henri de Montesquieu, aided by his son Hubert and his son-in-law Patrick Baseden, makes wines of indisputable quality that sells at reasonable prices. The range includes only wines from Graves, and the sweet white is harmonious, fruity, and lengthy. It is bottled in Bordeaux's traditional half-liter *fillettes,* and is packaged in equally traditional blue-painted wooden cases.

IDENTIFICATION

Type: sweet white wines.

Grape varieties: sémillon (73 percent), sauvignon (21 percent), muscadelle (6 percent).

Area: 1,092 acres (1994).

Production: Between 396,000 and 528,000 gallons on average.

Characteristics: Less sweet than *liquoreux* whites, these offer great finesse, with notes of wax and citrus fruits.

CHÂTEAU HAUT-BRION

The indisputable star of Pessac-Léognan, Graves, and indeed of all the Bordeaux *grands crus,* Haut-Brion found success early in its history and has never declined since. It all began on April 23, 1525, when Jean de Pontac married Jeanne de Bellon. Her dowry included land in Haut-Brion, part of the parish of Pessac. Eight years later, Jean de Pontac bought the noble house of Haut-Brion, officially giving birth to the estate. After having been married three times, Jean de Pontac died at the ripe old age of 101. His heirs undertook the expansion of the estate's area and the improvement of the quality of the wine. One of them was Arnaud II de Pontac, bishop of Bazas.

Arnaud III de Pontac, first president of the Bordeaux Parliament, had a marked influence on the history of Haut-Brion. In the 1660s, he improved vinification techniques, prolonged the barrel-aging of the wine for two or three years, and racked and topped off the wines regularly. He was also one of the first to sell his wine in London using the estate name (Pontac or Haut-Brion) rather than a generic appellation. Haut-Brion (sometimes spelled Aubrion) is even cited by the famous English diarist Samuel Pepys, who discovered it in an English tavern in 1663. Although he spelled it "Ho-Bryan," he was impressed enough by its particularly good taste to note it in his journal.

In 1694, after the death of Arnaud III de Pontac's son, the estate was divided into two parts, with the smaller one taking the name of Chai-Neuf. Haut-Brion then passed through the hands of several different owners, including Talleyrand, before it became the property of an important Bordeaux family, the Larrieus, in 1836. They bought Chai-Neuf in 1840 and reunited the two parts of the original estate. Three generations later, the law on jointly held property forced the Larrieu heirs to sell Haut-Brion, which was then managed by a company. In 1935, the company became the property of an American banker, Clarence Dillon, father of an American ambassador to France, who chose it over Cheval-Blanc. A new era of prosperity began with the arrival of the Dillon family. Joan, the granddaughter of Clarence Dillon, first married Prince Charles of Luxembourg, then, after his death, the Duc de Mouchy, in 1978. The couple still manages the estate.

Set on two hilltops, Douze and Bahans, in Graves, Haut-Brion is completely surrounded by the town of Pessac and Bordeaux's urban sprawl —a location must unusual for a vineyard of this calibre. With a total area of 116 acres, the estate devotes 109 acres to red wine (fifty-two percent cabernet sauvignon, thirty-three percent merlot, and fifteen percent cabernet franc) and 7 acres to white wine (sixty-three percent sémillon and thirty-seven percent sauvignon), for an average annual production of 200,000 to 245,000 bottles.

One of Haut-Brion's claims to fame is that it is the only vineyard outside the Médoc to be included in the classification of 1855. It was ranked as one of the four *premiers grands crus* of the era, along with Lafite, Latour, and Margaux. It was also included in the Graves classification a century later—only its red wine, that is, since no whites were produced there at the time.

Haut-Brion's location within the city protects it from the danger of freezes, allowing a harvest of fully ripened grapes. As it ages, the red wine develops smoky, spicy aromas that distinguish it from all others. Less robust than other *premiers crus classés,* it has great finesse, an incomparable silkiness, and an exciting complexity. The second wine, a red called Bahans-Haut-Brion, is highly appreciated by experts.

Also located in the town, opposite Haut-Brion, is Mission Haut-Brion, which has belonged to the heirs of Clarence Dillon since 1983. Although it wasn't ranked in the 1855 classification, this estate has been renowned for generations. Its name comes from the mission's congregation of priests, Vincentian monks who took possession of the

Haut-Brion, the oldest of the **grands crus** *in the Bordeaux region. Once situated in the countryside, it is now surrounded by urban sprawl.*

property in 1664. They worked hard to expand the vineyard and improve the wine, bringing it worldwide fame nearly as great as that of the wines of Haut-Brion. Nationalized during the French Revolution, the estate continued to prosper, especially when under the ownership of the Chiapella family. It currently has forty-nine acres planted with cabernet sauvignon (fifty percent), merlot (forty percent), and cabernet franc (ten percent). Its production is around 100,000 bottles per year. With perhaps a little less finesse than Haut-Brion, it has a good tannic constitution and a remarkable red-fruit bouquet.

The Château Laville-Haut-Brion, another *cru classé,* belongs to the Domaine Clarence Dillon. It is a small estate of less than ten acres. Run by La Mission Haut-Brion, it produces a superb dry white wine, most of which is exported. It can be aged as long as ten years before it begins to reveal its opulence and remarkable aromas.

Finally, there is La Tour Haut-Brion, another *cru classé* belonging to the Domaine Clarence Dillon. This twelve-acre estate is located near La Mission and produces a red wine with smoky aromas similar to those of Haut-Brion.

The various vineyards carrying the name Haut-Brion have the remarkable ability to produce excellent wines in the midst of a city.

Pessac-Léognan

Once known as Hautes-Graves, the local appellation Pessac-Léognan, created in September 1987, owes a great deal to the tenacity of one man, André Lurton, owner of several highly reputed vineyards in the Bordeaux region. After more than twenty years of effort, he finally obtained recognition by way of an appellation that includes Mérignac, Pessac, Talence, Canéjan, Cadaujac, Gradignan, Léognan, Martillac, Saint-Médard-d'Eyrans, and Villenave-d'Ornon, grouping fifty-five châteaux and estates.

In 1934, the INAO had already recognized the singularity of the Pessac and Léognan areas, according them the status of an authorized denomination but not an appellation.

History certainly justifies the distinction of this area in the heart of the Graves appellation. This is where the clarets that made Bordeaux famous as early as the middle ages were first produced, and all the estates listed in the 1959 classification of Graves are located in Pessac-Léognan.

The land itself, however, also played a vital role in this ranking. It consists of a group of gravelly hills perfectly suited for winegrowing, with steep hillsides that enable good drainage. Farther to the south, the undulating terrain has a larger marl content.

While the number of vineyards is limited in this region, the wines have strong personalities and have achieved great fame. The quality of Pessac-Léognan wines has continually improved since its official recognition. However, Pessac-Léognan vineyards, it must be noted, are still allowed to cite on their labels the origins of the wine in Graves.

Pessac-Léognan takes up twenty-five percent of the area of Graves, but represents fifty percent of the district's financial value.

• Bouscaut. Despite its eighteenth-century style, the château is actually recent. It was rebuilt in the 1960s after two fires ravaged the buildings, while sparing the *chais*. Since 1979, the family of Lucien Lurton, the brother of André Lurton, has been upholding the high quality of the estate's wines. Ninety-one acres are devoted to red wines, and twenty acres to whites.

• Carbonnieux. With 111 acres, this very old estate, which was known as early as 1234, is one of the largest producers of white wines. An anecdote dating from the period when the Benedictines of Sainte-Croix ran the estate recounts that they wanted to sell their wine in Turkey. Knowing that the consumption of alcohol is prohibited by the Koran, they called their product "mineral water from Carbonnieux in Guienne." Afterward, Carbonnieux was more or less forgotten until 1956, when the Perrins took it in hand. The estate now produces more highly concentrated whites thanks to the introduction of barrel aging. Red wine is produced in almost the same quantity as white, but it is less well known.

• Domaine de Chevalier. Once called Chibaley, this former farm became a

IDENTIFICATION

Type: red and white wines.

Grape varieties: Reds: cabernet sauvignon (39 percent), merlot (48 percent), cabernet franc (13 percent); Whites: sémillon (73 percent), sauvignon (21 percent), muscadelle (6 percent).

Area: Reds: 2,208 acres; whites: 482 acres (1994).

Production: Reds: 1.3 million gallons on average; whites: 343,200 gallons on average.

Characteristics: The reds are distinguished by a their fruity bouquet and good structure and balance. The whites offer great aromatic richness that is fresh and fatty.

vineyard in 1863, when Jean Ricard inherited it from his father. Jean was a cooper, and he transformed the large farm into a fine vineyard that produces wines of an increasingly high quality. He also became owner of Fieuzal and Naudet, and he married a woman who owned Malartic-

Olivier Bernard presides over the destiny of the celebrated Domaine de Chevalier.

Lagravière. His social ascension was unusual for the time, and he even became mayor of Léognan, where he had several communal buildings constructed. In the twentieth century, his daughter and his son-in-law, Gabriel Beaumartin, continued the work of Jean Ricard. Today, on eighty-seven acres, Olivier Bernard produces red wines that are remarkable for their pronounced bouquet and their consistency. The whites, known as some of the best in the area for their floral aroma and their powerful structure, are produced in small quantities and grown on only ten acres of land.

• Couhins. This 124-acre estate is unusual in that it has been run since 1979 by the Institut national de la recherche agronomique. The estate is located less than four miles from the institute's laboratories, and its forty-five acre vineyard (whose whites are classified) is used for research on vines and wine. Only part of the harvest, vinified in the traditional way, has the right to the appellation. A twenty-acre parcel is rented by the Lurton family, which produces an excellent white wine (*cru classé*) under the name Couhins-Lurton.

• Fieuzal. Instead of the place-name Fieuzal, this estate might well have taken the name La Rochefoucauld, as it belonged to this famous family for many years. "I see sobriety as a form of impotence," wrote François de La Rochefoucauld, the celebrated seventeenth-century writer and moralist. The estate had its ups and downs afterward, before being brought up to par during the Empire by Alfred de Griffon (which explains the imperial insignia of the bee on the cap-

sules), and then by Jean Ricard at the end of the nineteenth century. Only its red wines, with their richness and good breeding, were classified in 1959, but Fieuzal was one of the pioneers in the raising of the standard for white wines in the 1980s. Today, the estate's whites are its best known and most expensive product, even though they are produced in very small quantities.

• France. Run by the energetic Bernard Thomassin for a few years now, this unclassified estate located near Fieuzal has shown great improvement. Located a couple of miles from the Montesquieu manor, the vineyard stretches over the lovely hills of Graves. The reds are powerful and should not be drunk until they have aged for a few years to ensure that the aromas are balanced and well-blended with the wood.

• Haut-Bailly. This *cru classé,* which produces only red wines, was strongly influenced in the nineteenth century by Alcide Bellot des Minières. After he built the château and developed the vineyard, he began to produce wines of such high quality that they sold at the same prices as the best wines of the Médoc. Between the two world wars, the estate became the property of a geographer, Frantz Malvesin, who experimented with pasteurizing wine. Then, after years of being almost completely abandoned, Haut-Bailly was purchased by the Sanders family, which restored the estate's quality and fame by making noble, well-balanced wines.

• Haut-Gardère. Over a period of fifteen years, Jacques Lésineau succeeded in raising the level of this estate, which has since been taken over by its neighbor Fieuzal.

• La Louvière. Owned by André Lurton's family, this unclassified vineyard is well known for both its whites and reds, which are seen as being perfectly representative of the Pessac-Léognan style. La Louvière's second wine, called "L," is vinified in the same way as the first wine, but doesn't have its power. Still, it is a charming wine in its simplicity and lack of pretension. André Lurton's other

WINE LABELS

This label from a bottle of 1921 Carbonnieux red wine shows how the vineyards located in Pessac and, in this

case, Léognan, sought to identify themselves with a more precise origin than just Graves. At the time, there were no regulations on the subject.

It is interesting to note that the wine was identified as a *premier cru supérieur,* although no such classification formally yet existed.

vineyards are just as interesting and, being less well known, their wines can be had for reasonable prices. They are Couhins Lurton, which makes only whites; Cruzeau, whose reds are exceptional in certain years; and Rochemorin, a property that once belonged to Montesquieu, with fine white wines and likable reds.

• Malartic-Lagravière. In 1803, Pierre de Malartic, a descendant of a family known for fighting alongside General Montcalm in Quebec, added his name to that of the Lagravière estate. This *cru classé* belonged to one after another of the well-known families in the region, including the Ricards, the Ridorets, and the Marlys, before becoming the property of the Champagne house, Laurent-Perrier. One of the Marlys, Bruno, still manages the thirty-five acres of reds and ten acres of whites, producing wines that are truly representative of the appellation, known for their balance and finesse.

• Olivier. Part of this amazing château dates from the thirteenth century and is a classified historic monument. The orangerie and a good part of the estate (with a total area of 519 acres) are just as ancient. Vines have been grown here for a long time. One of the estate's many owners was the father of Montesquieu, the famous eighteenth-century writer. Olivier now belongs to Jean-Jacques de Bethmann. It produces red wines on seventy-four acres and whites on thirty-seven acres. The whites are made by the oenologist Denis Dubourdieu, a specialist in white wine.

• Pape-Clément. This estate was named after Bertrand de Goth, the archbishop of Bordeaux, who was elected pope in 1305 and took the name Clément V. He is best known for banning the Templars. The estate remained church property until the French Revolution, and the neo-Gothic château dates from the end of the nineteenth century. Located in Pessac, the estate was completely surrounded by the growing city and, like Haut-Brion, was only able to survive thanks to a devotion

to quality that has been continued by its successive owners. The proprietor today is Bernard Magrez, an important Bordeaux merchant. The red wine has a fine reputation, and it approaches the quality of Haut-Brion with its complex, smoky, spicy bouquet, and mellow, seductive structure. Seventy-four acres are devoted to red wine grapes. The estate also produces a small quantity of fine white wine.

• Picque-Caillou. Situated near the Mérignac airport, this is another estate that was able to stand up to the urban sprawl that encircled it by constantly improving quality. Its wines, most of them red, have an aromatic complexity that is close to that of Haut-Brion or Pape-Clément.

• Smith-Haut-Lafitte. The common Gironde name Lafite (or Lafitte) comes from the Gascon word *hite,* which means "small hill." In 1720, Georges Smith added his name to this estate, which has existed since at least 1549. Located in Martillac, this *cru classé* was managed, then owned for a long time by the trading house Eschenauer. It is now owned by Daniel Cathiard, who has gone all out to improve the quality of the wines, which had declined for some time. The vineyard is dominated by red wine grapes (111 acres). The wine is delicate but has a fine structure. There is also a small production of white wine, made exclusively with sauvignon grapes.

• Tour-Martillac (La). Named after a twelfth-century tower, this seventy-four-acre *cru classé* produces mainly red wines. The Kressmann family, also known for its trading activities in Bordeaux, has run the estate since 1880. The vines are among the oldest in the district, and hundred-year-old stock produces a small amount of white wine that is famous for its powerful, seductive aromas and superb finish.

The original label, with its gold and sand-colored stripes, was considered avant-garde when it was designed in 1929.

LIBOURNE AND BLAYE-BOURG

Libourne and Blaye-Bourg are two large Bordeaux winegrowing districts on the right bank of the Dordogne, with Libourne the major center. To the north are Blaye and Bourg, then, toward the southeast, Fronsac, Pomerol, and Saint-Émilion. At the confluence of the Dordogne and Isle rivers, Libourne has always been the natural port of the area and an important center for the wine trade. Many merchant houses are based there, and the city once rivaled Bordeaux as a trading center.

The Roman origins of the area's vineyards may be just a legend, but it is certain that wine played an important role here in the middle ages. The unity apparent in the Médoc and Graves areas is not the case here. Diversity reigns in Libourne and Blaye-Bourg, both in terms of landscapes and wines, which offer a wide range of styles and flavors. The same variety is found in the vines. Cabernet sauvignon is dominant on the opposite side of the Garonne, but this is the kingdom of merlot, which produces warm, seductive, and often well-rounded wines. The Libourne district and the Bordeaux region could almost be identified as two distinct winegrowing areas. Even the architecture is different—here you won't see châteaux like those found in the Médoc. But the unity of the Bordeaux region's vineyards rests on other factors: the concept of a *cru,* the practice of blending wines from different grape varieties, and a certain cultural approach.

Opposite: The famous Grandes Murailles, in the village of Saint-Émilion.
Above: Château Beauregard.

Saint-Émilion

According to tradition, it was here that the Romans planted the first vines. History tells us that the Latin poet Decimus Magnus Ausonius, known here as Ausone, was born in Bordeaux around A.D. 310. According to the writings of one of his friends, Paulin de Nole, one of Ausone's villas, Lucaniacus, was located in the Saint-Émilion area, but the exact location has never been determined. In 1843, a Roman villa was discovered in Saint-André-de-Montagne, near Saint-Émilion; more recently, Roman mosaics, some of them depicting vines, were found near the Château La Gaffelière. There is, however, little concrete proof that a vineyard existed on the site at the time.

The region's name comes from a monk named Émilian, from Vannes in Brittany, who established a retreat in the area in the seventh century. His reputation for wisdom attracted many pilgrims to the site. In the nineteenth century, the historian Émilien Piganeau came up with another possible explanation based on the place names used in the middle ages. *Sentmelion* or *Semilione,* from the Greek for "fountain of Semele," with its reference to the mother of Dionysius, would indicate the presence of vines. If this is the case, "Saint-Émilion" means "fountain amid the vines."

In the middle ages, the vine, although

IDENTIFICATION

Type: red wine.

Grape varieties: merlot (69 percent), cabernet franc (19 percent), cabernet sauvignon (12 percent).

Area: 13,550 acres (1994).

Production: 7.4 million gallons on average.

Characteristics: Full-bodied, well-structured wines, with a generous style.

already important, was just one agricultural activity among many; it is probable that mostly white wines were produced at the time. Some writings from the period call them *gentils.* Not being close to Bordeaux, Saint-Émilion was slow to attract investors to its vineyards and for a long time was cultivated in shareholdings.

The expansion of the vineyards and the production of red wines began around the end of the seventeenth century. Beginning in the eighteenth century, the demand from Dutch merchants for better-quality wines was a determining factor in this change. The relationship between Libourne and Blaye-Bourg on the one hand, and Bordeaux and the vineyards of the left bank, on the other, worsened as a result. The admiralty of Bordeaux, displeased by the growth of its rival, closed down the port of Libourne several times. A natural outlet for the wines of the area, the port did not become totally autonomous until 1739.

In the second half of the eighteenth century, a few pioneers, including Raymond Fontémoing (from a family of grain and salt merchants), Élie de Carle, Jacques Kanon, and the Sèze and Chaton-

Detail of one of the Roman mosaics found in the 1980s by the owner of Château La Gaffelière, Léo de Malet-Roquefort. The mosaics are vestiges of a Gallo-Roman palace dating to the fourth century.

net families, increased their efforts to improve quality. There are indications that a hierarchy was developing that differentiated between *primeur* and aged wines, and first and second class wines. A few names of owners appear in the records, but it wasn't until a century later that the word "château," as used in the Médoc to indicate the whole estate, came into more general use in the area.

The constant breaking up of estates and the recession that followed the Empire impaired efforts to improve quality, and Saint-Émilion was ignored by the classification of 1855. The area caught up during the next Exposition Universelle, in 1867, when thirty-eight of its *crus* were awarded a collective gold medal by the wine committee. This selection could have provided the basis for a classification, but it didn't happen at the time.

The winegrowers of Saint-Émilion were ahead of those in other areas when it came to selling their wines directly to consumers. This freed the producers from the grip of the merchants and contributed greatly to the international renown of the appellation, now famed throughout the world.

Divided among eight communities set around the city of Libourne, the terrain of Saint-Émilion is fairly heterogeneous, with a limestone plateau and clay-limestone soil to the north (the source of the best wines), a more gravelly area in the direction of Pomerol, and sandy alluvial deposits toward the south in the direction of the Dordogne. Saint-Émilion has a separate classification method (see pages 104-105), which complicates things for the beginner. But the appellation offers a number of good wines and *grands crus*, with two outstanding examples, Ausone and Cheval-Blanc, the only *premiers grands crus classés* (category A).

• Ausone. Unlike most estates in the region, Ausone has always remained in the hands of the same family. Currently managed by Mme. Dubois-Challon, it is jointly owned by her grand-nieces and great-nephews, the Vauthiers.

The estate dates to 1770, when Jean Cantenat, a master cooper, married Jeanne Chatonnet, whose family owned large amounts of property. It was an important estate at the time and had a château, constructed in 1781. Jean Cantenat chose to name the estate after the Latin poet Ausone, but for a long time the wine was known as *cru Cantenat, à la Madeleine,* after its locality.

The seventeen-acre Ausone estate has a beautiful setting and is divided into two distinct parts: a limestone plateau on one side and deep soil on the other. There are also two grape varieties, merlot and cabernet franc. The synthesis of these variations has long produced wine known for its high quality. Fine and supple when young, the wine develops an amazing complexity as it ages, with wide range of aromas. Mild and tender, it has a long, persistent finish that is enchanting.

• Cheval-Blanc. Named after its location, the estate was created in 1832 by Mr. Ducasse, who gradually expanded it to include a part of the once-huge Figeac estate, near Pomerol. The elegant château was built at about the same time. Beginning in 1853, Mr. Ducasse's son-in-law,

Jacques Fourcaud-Laussac, expanded the property until it reached 104 acres, with 89 acres of vines. He also installed a drainage system that was far ahead of its time. The estate is still owned by the heirs of Mr. Ducasse.

The soil—mostly sand and gravel, with iron slag underneath—and the grape varieties are atypical for the appellation. The decision, made long ago, to use mostly cabernet franc grapes resulted in a wine that is fine and elegant, fruity and fresh. But it takes about ten years of aging before a Château Cheval-Blanc reveals its sumptuous texture, unequaled sophistication, and long, distinguished finish. Although in a very different register, it reaches the level of Ausone in terms of quality and renown.

• L'Angélus. The name refers to the fact that this was the only place where the announcement of the Angelus could be heard ringing from the three local churches. Owned by the same family since the beginning of the twentieth century, the sixty-four-acre vineyard has improved appreciably since the 1980's. The reward came with its accession to the rank of *premier grand cru classé* in 1996.

• Beauséjour. The estate's name dates only to 1787. Its owner, General de Carle, preferred it to the former name, Puycoucou, for commercial reasons. In 1869, the estate was divided in half to settle inheritance claims. The resulting estates were Beauséjour Duffau-Lagarrosse (which still belongs to the same family) and Beau-Séjour Bécot (the name of the family that has owned it since 1969), which was expanded in 1979. Removed from the list of *premiers grands crus* in the 1986 classification, Beau-Séjour Bécot was restored to grace in 1996.

• Belair. The vineyard on this estate, which probably dates to the Gallo-Roman era, was created around 1750 by Jacques de Canolle (a French version of the English name Knolles). His descendants managed to hold on to the estate during the French Revolution and until 1916, when it was sold to the Dubois-Challon family, owners of Château Ausone.

• Canon. Already well-known in the eighteenth century, its wines are appreciated for their high level of consistency and quality.

• Figeac. This was already a great estate in the Gallo-Roman era under the name Figeacus and was later one of the most important wine estates in Saint-Émilion. Mistakes made by one of its owners, André de Carle-Trajet, who unwisely replaced some of the vines with crops such as clover and madder at the beginning of the nineteenth century, led to the ruin of the estate and forced his widow to break it up. It was then that Cheval-Blanc and other estates acquired parts of Figeac. Its atypical soil of gravel and sand (as in Médoc) is planted mostly with cabernets, which give its wines great finesse and distinguishes them from the other wines of the appellation.

WINE LABELS

This rather austere label from a 1924 Pavie is a model of clarity. At a time when no regulations governing the matter existed, it already provide all

the essential information. First, it names the château, important because a château in the Bordeaux region is a sort of commercial brand name and serves as a guarantee of quality to the consumer. Then it gives the appellation, which would not be officially established until twelve years later. And, finally, it also states the vintage year. There is no mention of the *cru classé* status, which was not inaugurated in Saint-Émilion until 1954.

• Clos-Fourtet. Entirely walled-in and situated near the town of Saint-Émilion, this estate attracts many visitors. It has a pleasant bourgeois house that was built before the French Revolution. It has been run since 1948 by the Lurton family.

• La Gaffelière. Built on the site of a former leper colony (a leper was called a *gaffet* in the middle ages), this is a very old estate. Gallo-Roman mosaics have been found there that include, among other things, a multicolored representation of a vine. Some believe that this was the site of the Latin poet Ausone's villa. La Gaffelière has belonged to the Malet-Roquefort family for several centuries, a guarantee of consistent quality.

• Magdelaine. The unusual spelling of the estate's name, which dates to the end of the nineteenth century, may have been invented to differentiate it from other places named Madeleine (including the location of Château Ausone). The twenty-five-acre vineyard, where merlot is the dominant grape variety (eighty-five percent), has been restored to its former glories since its purchase in 1952 by Jean-Pierre Moueix, a successful Libourne merchant.

• Pavie. Set on one of the most beautiful pieces of land in the area, this estate has grown and shrunk over the years, depending on its owners. It withstood the phylloxera epidemic thanks to an ingenious (and costly) system of spraying carbon sulfide from the top of the hill.

• Trottevieille. The estate's name comes from a sixteenth-century legend, which recounts that an old lady *(vieille)* who lived there was in the habit of trotting down the hill to hear the news from the passing stagecoach. The vineyard has belonged to the trading house Borie-Manoux since 1949.

The *grands crus classés* are of mixed quality, but can often be had for reasonable prices. There are also excellent discoveries to be made in the rest of the appellation.

Château Cheval-Blanc (right) and Château Ausone are the only two **premiers grands crus** *in category A. Cheval-Blanc was built in 1834 by Mr. Ducasse, founder of the vineyard.*

THE CLASSIFICATION OF SAINT-ÉMILION WINES

The similar names of some of the Saint-Émilion wines can cause confusion. First of all, it is important to know that there are two *appellations d'origine contrôlées,* Saint-Émilion and Saint-Émilion Grands Crus.

The relationship is similar to that of Bordeaux to Bordeaux Supérieurs. (See the chapter entitled "The Regional Appellations.") Saint-Émilion Grands Crus are selected after a second approval tasting and must meet more stringent quality requirements than Saint-Émilion wines. In spite of this, there are more Saint-Émilion Grands Crus than Saint-Émilions in terms of both area (8,494 acres for the former and 5,056 acres for the latter) and volume (4.2 million gallons and 3.2 million gallons, respectively).

Among the Saint-Émilion Grands Crus, whose number can vary from year to year, there is a further ranking. Established in 1955, this classification is revised every ten years, unlike the other classification systems in the Bordeaux region, which is a cause of some dissension.

The last revision took place in 1996. The committee (whose composition may be different each time) consisted of nine members nominated by the Saint-Émilion winegrowers association and chosen by the Institut national des appellations d'origine (INAO): two wine brokers, a merchant, an oenologist, three professors, and a legal adviser, and the honorary president of the INAO. In addition to submitting a complete file on each vineyard presented (primarily made up of a list of the wine's prices over the preceding ten years), the estates had to meet several criteria to merit their classification:

- The wine must have used the same estate name for the past ten years.
- The wine sheds, or *chais,* must have been used only for the wines of the estate.
- At least fifty percent of the vines must have been twelve or more years old.
- At least seven of the last ten harvests must have been designated *grands crus.*
- The wine must have been bottled on the estate.

Ratified by the INAO, the 1996 classification includes thirteen *premiers grands crus classés* (two in category A and eleven in category B) and fifty-five *grands crus classés* (which should not be confused with the Saint-Émilion appellation's *grand cru*). The committee promoted Beau-Séjour Bécot and L'Angélus to the status of *premiers grands crus*, and named as *grands crus* Cadet-Bon, Grandes Murailles, Laroque, and La Couspaude. No fewer than twelve vineyards were eliminated from the list altogether.

Such classifications are always subject to criticism, and some feel that too many vineyards are selected (but it must not be forgotten that Saint-Émilion is a large region). Others do not agree with the use of two categories (A and B) for the *premiers grands crus classés*. Still others object that tasting is not the primary, or even the only, criterion. Yet for beginners, this classification is a useful tool. And we should congratulate the wine producers of Saint-Émilion, who are willing to have their classifications reviewed every ten years, while other estate owners consider their rankings as inalterable, an unrealistic position given the ongoing changes taking place on many estates.

Premiers grands crus classés

A

- Ausone
- Cheval-Blanc

B

- l'Angélus
- Beau-Séjour Bécot
- Beauséjour Duffau-Lagarrosse
- Belair
- Canon
- Clos Fourtet
- Figeac
- La Gaffelière
- Magdelaine
- Pavie
- Trottevieille

Grands crus classés

- Balestard la Tonnelle
- Bellevue
- Bergat
- Berliquet
- Cadet-Bon
- Cadet-Piola
- Canon-La Gaffelière
- Cap de Mourlin
- Chauvin
- Clos des Jacobins
- Clos de l'Oratoire
- Clos Saint-Martin
- Corbin
- Corbin-Michotte
- Couvent des Jacobins
- Curé Bon La Madeleine
- Dassault
- Faurie de Souchard
- Fonplégade
- Fonroque
- Franc-Mayne
- Grand-Mayne
- Grand-Pontet
- Grandes Murailles
- Guadet-Saint-Julien
- Haut-Corbin
- Haut-Sarpe
- Lamarzelle
- Laniote
- Larcis Ducasse
- Larmande
- Laroque
- Laroze
- L'Arrosée
- La Clotte
- La Clusière
- La Couspaude
- La Dominique
- La Serre
- La Tour du Pin Figeac (Giraud-Bélivier)
- La Tour du Pin Figeac (Moueix)
- La Tour Figeac
- Le Prieuré
- Matras
- Moulin du Cadet
- Pavie-Decesse
- Pavie-Macquin
- Petit-Faurie-de-Soutard
- Ripeau
- Saint-Georges Côte-Pavie
- Soutard
- Tertre-Daugay
- Troplong-Mondot

The Saint-Émilion Satellites

(Lussac, Montagne, Puisseguin, Saint-Georges)

The communities of Lussac, Montagne, Puisseguin, Sables, and Saint-Georges, under the jurisdiction of Saint-Émilion, used to sell their wines under the Saint-Émilion appellation. But owners whose estates were actually located in Saint-Émilion were concerned about the image of their wine and lobbied for the attribution of separate appellations to these communities. The château owners in those communities, in turn, were not happy with their new status. They demanded and obtained the right to add the illustrious name of Saint-Émilion to their respective appellations. Later, Sables was returned to the Saint-Émilion appellation, while Parsac and Saint-Georges were attached to Montagne-Saint-Émilion. But this did not put an end to the Parsac-Saint-Émilion and Saint-Georges-Saint-Émilion appellations. While the former is disappearing, the latter is still used.

The upshot of all this is that there are currently four appellations, all of them located to the northeast of Saint-Émilion. Their geographic proximity, as well as the soils (of great variety) and the style of the wines amply justify their assimilation. An argument could even be made that the four appellations should be united into one.

IDENTIFICATION

Type: red wine.

Grape varieties: merlot (69 percent), cabernet franc (19 percent), cabernet sauvignon (12 percent).

Area: 9,337 acres (1994).

Production: 5.8 million gallons on average.

Characteristics: Deeply colored, full-bodied, well-structured wines, very close cousins of those of Saint-Émilion.

Montagne and Lussac have about the same surface area, with 3,705 acres and 3,409 acres respectively, far more than Puisseguin (1,803 acres) and Saint-George (420 acres). As in Saint-Émilion, the estates are often small because of the gradual division of the vineyards over the centuries. Furthermore the topography of the area, with many hills topped with handsome houses, does not lend itself to large estates. The quality of the wines varies widely, but experts are generally in agreement that Montagne's wines are characterized by their fruitiness, Puisse-

guin's by their finesse, and Lussac's by their richness. There is no classification, and most experts agree that there are few dominant vineyards among these appellations. However, a few châteaux deserve special mention: Mayne Blanc, whose *cuvée spéciale* comes from old vines; Trocard, which belongs to the president of the Syndicat des Bordeaux et Bordeaux Supérieurs; La Grenière, for its barrel-aged cuvées; Croix-Beauséjour; Moulin-Noir, a new vineyard that is nevertheless highly recommended; Tricot, which uses traditional vinification methods; and Saint-André Corbin. Most of these Saint-Émilion satellites make pleasant, likable wines. They should be drunk between the ages of two and five years and offer good value for their price. They may not be in the big leagues, buy they can still be delightful.

Pomerol

The international fame of Pomerol is disproportionate to the small size of the area, and the rarity of the wines guarantees elevated prices on the market. Vineyards have existed here for a long time, but they were relatively unknown for centuries. In the middle ages, the Hospitallers of Saint-Jean-de-Jérusalem helped to increase the renown of the wine, but the Hundred Years' War all but destroyed the vineyards, which were not replanted until the sixteenth century.

The Pomerol craze began in the second half of the nineteenth century, aided by several clever wine merchants, many of them from Corrèze, including Janoueix and Moueix. Pomerol has great powers of seduction and relies on the roundness of merlot grapes, which are better expressed here than in other areas of the Bordeaux region. The wines open up sooner than those of the Médoc, but they can also be laid down for a long time.

In spite of its small size, the appellation has diverse soils, including a plateau of clay that contains some gravel and sand and, to the west, sandier soil. The estates are small and broken up into parcels. Few are larger than twenty-five acres. The quality and fame of some of its vineyards have been such that the area hardly needed an appellation. Over the past century, prices have risen to the point where there is hardly any hope of finding a good Pomerol at a reasonable price, except perhaps when it is purchased young.

IDENTIFICATION

Type: red wine.

Grape varieties: merlot (80%), cabernet franc (15%), cabernet sauvignon (5%).

Area: 1,934 acres (1994).

Production: 1.3 million gallons on average.

Characteristics: Powerful and warm, these are full-bodied wines with the characteristic aroma of truffles. They can be drunk relatively young, but they also age very well.

- Pétrus. Along with Yquem, these are the most expensive wines of the Bordeaux region, especially for older vintages. The estate covers twenty-seven acres, almost exclusively planted with merlot grapes, and its clay soil has good exposure to the sun. Pétrus has become a collector's, even a speculator's item, but, first and foremost, it is a great wine: rich, aromatic, and ample, with the flavor of truffles. Average production is between 30,000 and 40,000 bottles, but it is sometimes lower or, as in 1991, completely declassified. The vines and the vinification are lovingly supervised by the owners, the Moueix family. They are also merchants who know how to sell their wine throughout the world, especially on the American market, for which a part of the production is always reserved, especially in years with limited harvests. The harvest takes place in the afternoon to avoid any dilution of the wine caused by dew clinging to the grapes. It is completed within a few days to ensure that the grapes have arrived at the same level of maturity. Pétrus is so confident of its supremacy that "château" is not even added to its name.

- Lafleur. The production here is small, and the mix of grape varieties is unusual, with fifty percent cabernet franc. Because of this, many experts prefer Château Lafleur to Pétrus in some vintages because it can offer, in addition to its richness, a bit more finesse and nuance.
- La Conseillante. Along with its neighbors Pétrus and Cheval-Blanc, this is one of the glories of Pomerol. It has been owned by Nicolas for more than a century. The mix of grape varieties includes thirty-five percent cabernet, grown on soil of clay, gravel, and sand, which give the wine its complexity and long life span.
- Certan de May de Certan. Like Vieux Château Certan (founded in the sixteenth century by a Scottish family), this high-quality producer is on the Certan plateau.
- L'Évangile. When the Rothschilds of Lafite take such an interest in a vineyard that they buy shares in it, there must be a good reason. The wine from this estate is considered by many to be one of the most representative of the appellation.

Only a few privileged visitors ever see the dining room at Pétrus.

• La Fleur Pétrus. As its name indicates, this estate is located between two of the greatest Pomerol vineyards. Its soil, however, is not quite as good, making for wines that are less complex.

• Latour à Pomerol. A small tower gives its name to this estate, another property of the Moueix family. It is one of the classics of the appellation, with great consistency.

• Trotanoy. A neighbor of Pétrus, this is one of its most ambitious rivals. It also belongs to the Moueix family and benefits from very old vines that were spared from the freezes that ravaged Pomerol in 1956. Its soil, with a high clay content, creates wines that are both powerful and elegant.

• Gazin. With fifty-nine acres, this is one of the largest estates in Pomerol. The quality of its wines improved dramatically when mechanized harvesting was abandoned.

The land around Pomerol is flat, and the vineyards are divided into many small parcels.

Lalande-de-Pomerol

The little Bardanne River, which once marked the border between the *langue d'oc* and the *langue d'oïl* (the language groups of southern and northern France, respectively), separates the appellations Lalande-de-Pomerol and Pomerol. Founded by the Hospitallers of Saint-Jean-de-Jérusalem, the former uses similar grape varieties and has similar soil to the latter, yet the prices of the Lalande-de-Pomerol wines are much lower. The experts agree, however, that the best wines of the appellation are just as good as some Pomerols. This is a the place to look for good buys.

Two communities located on either side of the N89 roadway, Lalande-de-Pomerol and Néac, share the appellation, which was known as Néac before becoming Lalande-de-Pomerol, with its more commercial ring. Over the past few years, the winegrowers have been improving the quality of their product, with results that are increasingly apparent and appreciated, and sometimes spectacular.

• Garraud. This large estate (seventy-nine acres) benefits from old vines, yield control, grape selection, and partial aging in wood. This is one of the appellation's best bets.

• Grand Ormeau. Since it was purchased by Jean-Claude Beton, the former owner of Orangina, this vineyard's quality has continually improved. The caber-

IDENTIFICATION

Type: red wine.

Grape varieties: merlot (80 percent), cabernet franc (15 percent), cabernet sauvignon (5 percent).

Area: 2,705 acres (1994).

Production: 1.3 million gallons on average.

Characteristics: Much like the Pomerols, these wines are both powerful and supple, with a strong bouquet.

net grapes (thirt-five percent) add complexity to a rich, full-bodied wine.

• Bertineau Saint-Vincent. This small ten-acre estate benefits from the care of Michel Rolland, one of the Bordeaux region's great wine-makers.

• La Fleur Saint-Georges. Recently acquired by the insurance company AGF, this vineyard will now have the means to move upscale.

• Viaud. This is one of the few stars of the Lalande-de-Pomerol appellation, although experts are not always in agreement about its qualities.

• Samion. With only 0.7 acres, this tiny estate produces less than 2,000 bottles per year of high-quality wine.

• Les Hauts-Conseillants. With land in both Néac and Lalande-de-Pomerol, this vineyard is owned by a Pomerol estate, which shows in its vinification.

Fronsac and Canon-Fronsac

Overlooking the Dordogne River, Fronsac has dramatic landscapes, with two small hills that offer magnificent views of the surroundings. A fortress was built here in the time of Charlemagne, an indication of the region's strategic location.

The vineyards are very old, as in the rest of Libourne, and merlot grapes play a much larger role than the cabernets. The Fronsac appellation encompasses six communities and has 2,058 acres of vines, but only a few vineyards in two areas (Fronsac and Saint-Michel-de-Fronsac) are entitled to the other appellation, Canon-Fronsac. They must be located on hillsides with primarily clay-limestone soil. This second *appellation d'origine contrôlée,* with an area of around 741 acres, might be termed the elite of Fronsac, where there is no specific classification.

Fronsac is the forgotten wine of Libourne, but its power and elegance can rival some of the wines of Pomerol and Saint-Émilion. A new generation of winegrowers is striving to bring out the best in these often-powerful wines. With aging, they reveal much charm and elegance, offering high quality for their price.

Common practices here include the use of biodynamics (an increasingly popular method that respects the natural cycles of the vine), the restricted use of chemical products, and the thinning out of the vine's leaves, proving that it is always possible to improve the quality of an appellation, as long as the means are there.

The following are distinguished representatives of the Canon-Fronsac appellation.

• Barrabaque, whose good hillside exposure makes for wines that are more supple than those of the rest of the appellation.

• Canon, Canon de Brem, and Canon-Moueix are three small estates that belong to Jean-Pierre Moueix of Libourne. The wines are typical of the appellation and can be aged two to three years.

• Cassagne Haut-Canon. The owner, Jean-Jacques Dubois, is one of the pioneers in the improvement of the appellation's quality. An increased proportion of cabernets adds to the liveliness of the wine. The special reserve, La Truffière, is full-bodied and aromatically complex.

IDENTIFICATION

Type: red wine.

Grape varieties: merlot (69 percent), cabernet franc (19 percent), cabernet sauvignon (12 percent)
Area: 2,791 acres (1994).

Production: 1.5 million gallons on average.

Characteristics: Elegant and full-bodied, these are powerful wines that, when aged, can reveal fairly complex aromas, sometimes marked by the odor of truffles.

• Grand Renouil. On thirty acres, Michel Ponty makes one of the appellation's most successful wines, making good use of the assets of the merlot grapes.

• La Fleur Cailleau. Along with Château La Grave, this is one of the two properties owned by Paul Barre, a pioneer in the use of biodynamics in the region. The wine is well rounded, with a superb bouquet and controlled power.

• Moulin Pey-Labrie. Purchased in 1988 by wine lovers from the north of France, who followed the advice of the best oenologists in the region, the estate has since continually improved in quality. The wine has a personality that sets it apart in the region.

The following Fronsac vineyards are deserving of attention.

• De Carles. The château is handsome, and the wine is highly aromatic and can be laid down for a few years.

• Dalem. The wine is dark, almost black, and has great power and body. It is one of the classics of the appellation. It has been owned for more than forty years by Michel Rullier, who has worked hard to make Fronsac better known.

• La Dauphine. Another excellent wine, with both vigor and suppleness. The estate has belonged to the Moueix family since 1981 and is another testament to their skill in winemaking.

• La Vieille Cure. Owned by an American financial group, this vineyard on a

Saillans hillside is highly consistent and aromatically complex.

• Fontenil. This is the family property of Michel Rolland, the best-known oenologist in Libourne. Here he applies the methods that have made him famous in the region.

• Moulin Haut-Laroque. Typical of Fronsac, this vineyard benefits from old vines (a third of them are more than sixty-five years old), which give the wine a wonderful aromatic complexity.

• Renard Mondésir. Although the first part of this name normally means "fox," here it refers to a type of soil, white with limestone, that is unique to this seventeen-acre estate. The wine is distinguished by its powerful aromas.

Côtes de Castillon

Between Saint-Émilion and the eastern border of the Gironde department, the vineyards of Côtes de Castillon were for a long time some of the least known of the Bordeaux region. The small fortified city of Castillon-la-Bataille on the Dordogne River was itself famous for being the site of Charles VII's victory, which marked the end of the Hundred Years War in 1453.

The area resembles Saint-Émilion in many ways: similar landscapes, exposure to the sun, clay-limestone soil (especially in the eastern part), and grape varieties (predominantly merlot). But for a long time, the winegrowers were content to produce light wines without much character, and most of them were sent to merchants, who preferred quantity to quality and used the area's wines in their highly sellable blends of generic Bordeaux wines. This policy also served to preserve the hierarchy that protected more prestigious vineyards.

The situation began to change in the 1980s. The skyrocketing prices of the *grands crus* made them inaccessible to many consumers, who were often seeking out wines of character that expressed their origins rather than just looking for prestigious labels. Generic Bordeaux wines were no longer able to meet their expectations and were being supplanted by low-priced wines from other regions.

Many growers in the area understood that they could play a more important role by taking a chance on quality and honesty. In 1989, the Côtes-de-Castillon appellation was created. It encompasses nine communities: Belvès-de-Castillon, Castillon-la-Bataille, Saint-Magne-de-Castillon, Gardegan-et-Tourtirac, Saint-Colombe, Saint-Genès-de-Castillon, Saint-Philippe-d'Aiguille, Les Salles, and Monbadon. To obtain the appellation, the winegrowers must meet rigorous production standards, such as limiting the number of vines to five thousand per hectare (2.47 acres), a target that must be met by the year 2010.

The first vintages produced since then have been deemed highly promising by the experts, and Castillon is now seen as a nursery in which those who love high-quality Bordeaux at reasonable prices will soon find what they are looking for.

A sure sign of success is that outside investors are coming into the area, including insurance groups and Spanish companies that are betting on the future of these wines. Also remarkable is the fact that half of the production in the area is realized by cooperatives. Among the better-known vineyards, the following can be cited: Lapeyronie belongs to the former owners of a Saint-Émilion estate who are applying the same methods here to make wines with a long aging capacity. Arthus makes rich, aromatic wines that are perfectly vinified. Belcier is one of the leaders of the appellation thanks to investments in quality made by its owner, MACIF. Blanzac has an eighteenth-century manor house and makes tannic wines. Cap de Faugères' owner is from the world of cinema and has invested substantially to improve the production process. Côte Montpezat has also benefited from major investments and produces a wine that is powerful and harmonious. Grand Tuillac has great exposure to the sun, and its owner, Mr. Lavigne, has begun aging in wood barrels. La Caresse, as its name indicates, makes wines that are tender and fruity. La Clairière Laithwaite has a redundant name (both words mean "glade," one in French and the other in Celtic languages) and a British owner who has been making fine wines for thirty years. Poupille is interesting for its good equipment and expertise. Puy-Landry has old vines that produce highly concentrated wines. Robin has well-exposed vineyards and makes wines that age well.

IDENTIFICATION

Type: red wine.

Grape varieties: merlot (69 percent), cabernet franc (19 percent), cabernet sauvignon (12 percent).

Area: 7,445 acres (1994).

Production: 4 million gallons on average.

Characteristics: Supple and fruity, these wines can reach a high degree of richness and finesse.

Côtes de Francs

Located north of Castillon and northeast of Saint-Émilion, Côtes de Francs is a tiny appellation spread across three communities—Francs, Saint-Cibard, and Tayac—that have some of the highest elevations in the Gironde. In spite of its small size, its soil is varied, with areas of limestone and clay. The appellation's full name, Bordeaux Côtes-de-Francs, is a reminder that, like Castillon, the vineyards once provided generic wine to the merchants before the owners began making efforts to set themselves apart.

The wines produced here are more tannic and structured than those of Castillon. Some Saint-Émilion winegrowers have had an influence in the area, instituting methods that foster making of *grands crus,* including the reduction of yields, harvesting when the grapes are fully ripe, and aging in wood barrels. Some of the growers who have helped to raise the level of the appellation since the 1980s are the Thienponts of Puygueraud, La Claverie, and Charmes Godart; Dominique Hébrard and Hubert de Bouard of Francs; and Patrick Valette of La Prade. The oenologist Michel Rolland is an adviser to Château Marsau, which was purchased by Jean-Marie Chadronnier a few years ago. The local cooperative, which had some difficulties at the beginning of the 1990s, produces the respected Cellier-des-Côtes-de-Francs. The appellation also produces, white wines in tiny amounts, (fifty-four acres in 1994). In the good years, some of these are vinified as sweet wines, but they are just a drop in the bucket when compared with those of Montravel and Bergerac, known for the quality of their sweet and *liquoreux* wines.

IDENTIFICATION

Type: red wine.

Grape varieties: merlot (69 percent), cabernet franc (19 percent), cabernet sauvignon (12 percent).

Production: 528,000 gallons on average.

Characteristics: These powerful, tannic, rich wines have a strong bouquet.

Côtes de Bourg

Located south of Blaye and overlooking the Dordogne and Garonne rivers, Bourg was almost certainly planted with vines in the Gallo-Roman era, as it was more suitable than the marshy land of the Médoc.

The proximity of the river removes nearly all risk of frost, and the sunny area has a clay-limestone soil that tends to produce powerful, tannic wines. The quality of its soil may have contributed to the delay that the Côtes-de-Bourg wines have experienced in achieving their potential. These highly tannic wines were regularly added to weaker wines from the Médoc or elsewhere to improve the blends of the merchants.

IDENTIFICATION

Type: red and white wine.

Grape varieties: Reds: merlot (70 percent), cabernet sauvignon (24 percent), cabernet franc (6 percent); Whites: ugni blanc (59 percent), colombard (28 percent), sémillon (9 percent), sauvignon (3 percent), muscadelle (1 percent).

Area: 9,134 acres (1994).

Production: 5.5 million gallons on average.

Characteristics: Deeply colored, the red wines are fruity and tannic, with red-fruit aromas. The dry whites have a fine bouquet.

The situation has changed a great deal since the beginning of the 1980s, as in many other appellations on the right bank of the Dordogne.

A few pioneers have led the way in realizing the potential of the wines of Bourg by limiting yields, for example, to avoid

Many of the Bordeaux vineyards grow on slopes.

The lovely landscape of Côtes-de-Bourg, at the confluence of the Garonne and Dordogne Rivers.

rough wines and holding off on the harvest until the grapes are fully ripe.

Aside from a tiny production of dry white wines that cover a few dozen acres, Côtes-de-Bourg wines are mostly reds, with a predominance of merlot grapes. The best of them can be aged for at least four to six years before revealing their best qualities.

Tayac and Roc de Cambes are the best-known estates of the appellation. Both of them have been taken in hand by top professionals—Tayac in 1960 and Roc de Cambes in the 1980s—who have made great efforts to improve their quality.

Some of the most reputed and representative vineyards of Côtes-de-Bourg are Brulesécaille (both reds and whites), Le Clos du Notaire, Falfas (farmed with biodynamic techniques), Haut-Macô, Macay, Mercier, Nodoz, Relais de la Poste, and Sauman. But there are many other discoveries to be made in this appellation, and at very reasonable prices, as the overall quality continues to improve.

In order to make them better known, the Blaye and Bourg appellations created a joint wine competition in 1977, called the International Wine Challenge; it is now one of the most important wine contests in the world. In 1997, 4,822 wine and spirit samples from thirty-two countries were entered. The gold medal winners then participate in a second competition, CIVART, which awards trophies to the winners in each category at Vinexpo, the biennial wine and spirits exhibition held in Bordeaux.

Côtes de Blaye and Premières Côtes de Blaye

Blaye, located between the Gironde and Charente-Maritime departments, is named after the small port city that was long protected by a citadel built by Vauban, a French military engineer. Apart from the riverside areas, the lovely landscape consists of hills and valleys dotted with handsome houses and small châteaux.

Vines have probably been cultivated here since the Gallo-Roman era, but the vineyards have never earned much of a reputation. The grapes were just one of many agricultural crops grown, and the wines were used for local consumption or sold to merchants looking for inexpensive wines to add to their blends. The most widespread activity was the making of white wines, which were distilled to make Cognac before its manufacture was limited to the Charente region only. This explains the still-common use of ugni blanc grapes, which often go into the making of an eaux-de-vie (or brandy) called *fine de Bordeaux,* whose limited production has been regulated since 1974.

IDENTIFICATION

Type: red and white wine.

Grape varieties: Reds: merlot (70 percent), cabernet sauvignon (24 percent), cabernet franc (6 percent); Whites: ugni blanc (59 percent), colombard (28 percent), sémillon (9 percent), sauvignon (3 percent), muscadelle (1 percent).

Area: 11,342 acres (1994).

Production: 6.3 million gallons on average.

Characteristics: Deeply colored, the red wines are rather rustic and are fruity and powerful. The dry whites are pale in color and refreshing.

Vineyards, once one agricultural crop among many others, are now the mainstay of Blaye.

Once again, the local winegrowers have begun to make efforts to improve quality, although these are more sporadic than in other appellations. This has caused complications in terms of appellations, as at least five new ones have been designated, including both reds and whites. These are more demanding in terms of grape varieties and winemaking methods, and while they are taking precedence over the old ones, they have not yet completely eliminated them.

Today, things are a bit clearer with two principal *appellations d'origine contrôlée:*

- Premières-Côtes-de-Blaye is composed mostly of red wines, with a small amount of whites (less than ten percent of the appellation). They must be made of the noble grape varieties of the Bordeaux region: merlot and cabernet for the reds, and sauvignon and sémillon for the whites.
- Côtes-de-Blaye is for whites made from ugni blanc and colombard. The soil is mixed, with some areas made up of sand and clay and others of limestone (called *gruppes* here), which is especially good for growing cabernets. The wines

also vary in terms of quality, and those who take the time to taste the wines of the many estates may make some reasonably priced discoveries. Vinosity and the straightforward taste are the distinctive characteristics of the best reds, while the whites are refreshing and unpretentious.

Only a few vineyards stand out in the appellation. Château Bertinerie in Cubnezais was completely renovated in the 1980s, and its reds, whites, and *cuvées de prestige* (Haut-Bertinerie) are excellent. Other good bets are the small estate Les Jonqueyres (reds only, with a strong presence of merlot), Charron, Duc de Tutiac (the label of the Hauts de Gironde cooperative), Loumède, and Roland La Garde.

BETWEEN THE GARONNE AND THE DORDOGNE

The Entre-deux-Mers region is a huge triangle of land formed by the Garonne and Dordogne rivers and the eastern border of the Gironde department. This vast geographic mass ends in the Ambès headlands, a silty promontory that has continually advanced over the centuries. The area's name, meaning "between two seas," is due to the fact that both rivers rise and fall with the tides. This is a picturesque land, with its hills and valleys and contrasting vineyards, meadows, and forests. Along with its abundance of monuments, including fortified châteaux, houses and mills, it has much to attract tourists. Because it was difficult to reach for many centuries, the area retained its ancient traditions longer than many other areas.

The Entre-deux-Mers vineyards take up 61,750 acres, around a quarter of the area of the Bordeaux region, and are highly varied. They produce most of the red and dry white wines sold under the Bordeaux and Bordeaux Supérieurs labels. The Entre-deux-Mers appellation itself is used only for dry white wines of superior quality. It is not uncommon for one estate to produce both red and white Bordeaux as well as an Entre-deux-Mers. All these wines are produced in the center of the area, while the edges are part of other appellations: Premières-Côtes-de-Bordeaux and Sainte-Foy-Bordeaux to the east; Graves-de-Vayres; and the sweet white and noble-rot white winemaking areas (Cadillac, Loupiac, Sainte-Croix-du-Mont, and Saint-Macaire) along the Garonne, facing their counterparts across the river in Sauternes and Barsac.

Opposite: Château Bonnet is an estate that can be counted on for quality in Entre-deux-Mers, one of the loveliest parts of the Gironde.

Entre-deux-Mers

Entre-deux-Mers differs from other wine-growing areas of the Bordeaux region in that its siliceous soil contains sand, clay, and *molasse,* as well as silt deposited by the wind. The soil is generally compact and difficult to work. A variety of wines are made here (red, rosé, white, and sparkling), but the Entre-deux-Mers appellation is reserved for dry white wines only.

Undulating landscapes covered with vines are called* croupes *by the people of the Bordeaux region.

IDENTIFICATION

Type: white wine.

Grape varieties: sémillon (58 percent), sauvignon (21 percent), muscadelle (10 percent), ugni blanc (9 percent), colombard (2 percent).

Area: 5,602 acres (1994).

Production: 3 million gallons on average.

Characteristics: Fresh and lively, these are very dry wines. As their name indicates, they are a perfect accompaniment to seafood.

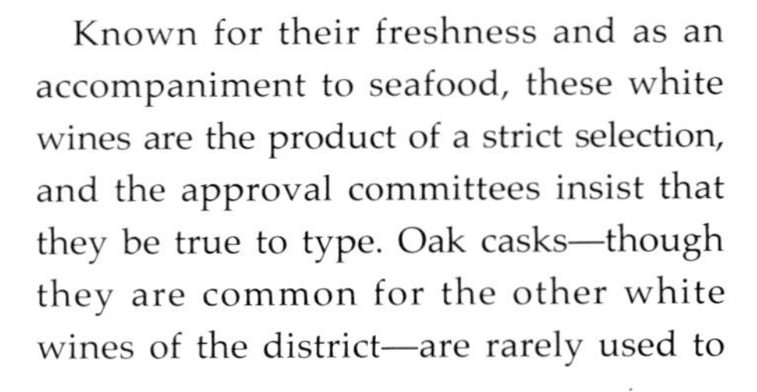

Known for their freshness and as an accompaniment to seafood, these white wines are the product of a strict selection, and the approval committees insist that they be true to type. Oak casks—though they are common for the other white wines of the district—are rarely used to

age them in a effort to preserve their freshness. They are perfumed by the characteristic bouquet and aromas of the sauvignon grape, which is used in varying proportions, depending on the estate. Since they are so carefully selected, the appellation's wines are generally very

well made from a technical point of view and have few defects. They are made to be drunk within a year. There are, however, variations from one estate to another, depending mostly on the grape varieties used.

Most of the estates here are family-

owned, yet they are often quite large. Château Bonnet, which belongs to André Lurton, is one example. This vineyard is a standard-setter for the appellation and has an area of 210 acres of vines for whites and 259 acres for reds. In spite of its size, it manages to produce highly consistent wines from one vintage to the next. Once again, André Lurton has done a fine job, as he has on the many other estates he owns in the Bordeaux region. The *cuvée réserve,* vinified in oak casks, has notes of vanilla and a varied bouquet.

Entre-deux-Mers wines can sometimes be vinified on the lees, which adds certain aromas and more opulence. A good example is the wine of Château Sainte-Marie, near Targon.

Other estates with unusual qualities include Château Haut-Pougnan, which uses ninety-five percent sauvignon grapes, and Château Haut-d'Arzac, whose wines are made with up to thirty-three percent muscadelle. The experts have also given the nod of approval Haut-Nadeau, La Mirandelle, La Mothe du Barry, and Mylord. But you can always count on Entre-deux-Mers wines because the standards of quality are strictly enforced by the appellation's committees, and the less-successful vintages and *crus* are more likely to be declassified than saved at any cost.

The district has a rising number of winegrowers who are practicing biodynamics, that is, growing the vines without fertilizers or chemical products, while respecting the natural life cycle of the plant.

Entre-deux-Mers-Haut-Benauge is a small, separate appellation (also used for red wines) that covers nine communities around the former Château de Benauge, not far from Cadillac. But its use is declining as winegrowers prefer to use the general appellation.

Premières Côtes de Bordeaux

Spreading from the city of Bordeaux as far as Cadillac (pretty much the capital of the appellation), the vineyards of Premières-Côtes-de-Bordeaux take up around thirty-seven miles along the banks of the Garonne. These old vineyards benefit from hillsides with excellent exposure to the sun and magnificent views over the Garonne valley. For a long time, this was a favorite spot for the vacation homes of well-to-do Bordeaux residents, and there are many fine properties in the area. Following in the footsteps of Toulouse-Lautrec, Anatole France, and François Mauriac, many celebrities have lived in and loved the area. And it is true that there is something special about this part of the Bordeaux region.

The soil is varied, with rich alluvial deposits, hillsides of gravel or limestone, and areas with clay underlayers. Such diversity allows for the making of many different types of wines, including red, white, rosé, light red, and sparkling wines. Many of them are sold under the corresponding regional appellations.

They are less well known than other wines of the Bordeaux region because they were traditionally used mostly as table wines by Bordeaux residents, who preferred to sell the more prestigious appellations of the Médoc or Libourne. The appellation began to shine only in the 1960s, when many French expatriates returned from Algeria and settled here.

In practice, the Premières Côtes de Bordeaux appellation is applied to red wine and to a small (less than 1,235 acres) production of whites, the best of which are mostly sold under the Cadillac appellation. The well-balanced red wines are highly representative of the "taste of Bordeaux," with a harmonious blend of richness and finesse, vinosity and lightness, plus a seductive, subtle woodiness.

Most of the wines of the appellation offer very good value, because they are almost always well made. It is rare to find a mediocre example. Since these wines are relatively unknown, the prices remain reasonable, and an amateur wine lover can make some superb discoveries. Some of the wines can be aged for a few years. Château Malagar, where François Mauriac and his family lived for decades, is an excellent vineyard with a small production of red wines (fifteen acres) that is acclaimed by many experts, some of whom even rate it among the best of the appellation.

Other names that can be counted on are Canteloup; the small Chelivette estate; Haux, whose wines are mostly exported to northern Europe by its Danish owners; Renon, renowned for its great consistency; Reynon, where owner Denis Dubourdieu, an oenologist, puts into practice the advice that he gives to other Bordeaux winegrowers; Sissan; Tanesse, which belongs to the Cordier estates; and Château Brethous, whose owners, Denise and François Verdier, have worked for many years to make the appellation better known.

Produit de France

1994

CHATEAU DE HAUX

PREMIERES COTES DE BORDEAUX

Appellation Premières Côtes de Bordeaux Contrôlée

S.C.A. DU CHATEAU DE HAUX

12%vol. Propriétaire à Haux (Gironde) 75cl.

MIS EN BOUTEILLES AU CHATEAU

IDENTIFICATION

Type: red and white wine.

Grape varieties: Reds: merlot (45 percent), cabernet sauvignon (33 percent), cabernet franc (22 percent); Whites: sémillon (73 percent), sauvignon (21 percent), muscadelle (6 percent).

Area: 8,149 acres (1994).

Production: 3.4 million gallons on average.

Characteristics: Deeply colored and full-bodied, the red wines are powerful yet fruity and have finesse. The whites range from sweet (*moelleux*) to noble-rotted sweet (*liquoreux*) wines.

The winegrowers of Premières Côtes de Bordeaux often use the appellation only for their *cuvées de prestige,* which are usually aged in wood, and sell the rest of their production under regional appellations. This is an effective way of increasing the quality of the appellation.

Côtes de Bordeaux Saint-Macaire is all the way to the south, east of Loupiac and Saint-Croix-du-Mont. It was once known for its sweet and noble-rotted sweet wines, but their production has declined to around 247 acres, while that of the red wines, sold under regional appellations, is increasing.

Graves de Vayres

This small appellation should not be confused with the winegrowing area on the left bank of the Garonne. It deserves its own appellation because of the exceptional presence of gravel soil in this area to the north of Entre-deux-Mers, tucked into a curve of the Dordogne across from Libourne. Only two villages, Vayres and Arveyres, are in the appellation.

Originally, only sweet and noble-rotted sweet white wines were produced in the area, but reds have been taking their place and now represent two-thirds of the production, much of it sold under regional appellations. Three estates that stand out are Haut-Mongeat, Lesparre (a large estate of ninety-nine acres), and Pichon Bellevue.

IDENTIFICATION

Type: red and white wine.

Grape varieties: Reds: merlot (70 percent), cabernet sauvignon (24 percent), cabernet franc (6 percent); Whites: sémillon (73 percent), sauvignon (21 percent), muscadelle (6 percent).

Area: 1,334 acres (1994).

Production: 792,000 gallons on average.

Characteristics: Deeply colored, the red wines are rustic and powerful yet fruity. The dry whites are pale and fresh.

THE INCREASINGLY RARE SAINTE-FOY-BORDEAUX

The Sainte-Foy-de-Bordeaux appellation, named after the town of Sainte-Foy-la-Grande, is in the far west of the department on the left bank of the Dordogne. In theory, it includes red wines as well as whites, which may be dry or sweet depending on the potential of the vintage. But this appellation is used less and less by estate owners, especially for reds, which are mostly sold under the Bordeaux and Bordeaux Supérieurs appellations. This trend toward the disappearance of regional appellations that do not have specific qualities is a result of the adaptation of Bordeaux winegrowers to market demands. The whites of this appellation are slightly more numerous.

SWEET WINES

Almost all of the noble-rot sweet white *(liquoreux)* appellations are found in the south of the Bordeaux region, on both sides of the Garonne River. This is because the area has a unique climate that is affected by the cold waters of a small river, the Ciron. In the autumn, its meeting with the warmer waters of the Garonne causes foggy mornings, which, followed by sunny afternoons, create a favorable environment for the growth of a certain type of mold, *Botrytis cinerea.* Normally, winegrowers fear this parasite because it causes gray rot, which can ruin an entire harvest, but in the special conditions of this area, the rot becomes "noble."

The concentrated juice of noble-rotted grapes is syrupy, and the production of *liquoreux* wines is difficult and time-consuming. Its production is not always possible if the weather has been too cold or rainy. Because the noble rot grows irregularly from one vine to another and even from one grape to another, the grapes must be picked selectively by hand and yields are very small. This explains why many winegrowers avoid making these problematic wines and prefer other types. Furthermore, these wines have a tendency to go in and out of fashion.

Aside from the most famous and highly regarded appellations, Sauternes and Barsac, there are Cérons, on the left bank of the river, and Cadillac, Loupiac, and Sainte-Croix-du-Mont on the right. Their finesse and aromatic qualities make them worth seeking out.

Opposite: Château de Suduiraut, one of the many handsome estates in Sauternes.
Above: Noble-rotted grapes are not pretty to look at, but they are essential to the making of liquoreux *wines.*

CHÂTEAU D'YQUEM

Laurent de Sauvage, one of the lords of Yquem. The château became the property of the family following the marriage of Françoise-Joséphine de Sauvage to Louis-Amédée de Lur-Saluces in 1785.

The best-known and probably most expensive vineyard in the Bordeaux region, Château d'Yquem produces an incomparable Sauternes. It was the only wine of its type to receive the designation *premier cru supérieur* in the classification of 1855.

The name Yquem has a curious etymology and is probably Germanic in origin. It contains the compound word *aighelm* (*aigan* means "to have" and helm means "helmet"), which is found in many first names beginning in the tenth century: Aichelmus, Akelmus, Ayquelmus, and Ayquem. The patronymic Eyquem, spelled this way since the sixteenth century, is fairly common in the Bordeaux region. Contrary to a persistent legend, Michel Eyquem de Montaigne has nothing to with Château d'Yquem. Like all the assets of the provost of Barsac, the estate belonged for some time to the kings of England (who were also the dukes of Aquitaine), then to the kings of France beginning in 1453. They had the land farmed in return for an annuity. In 1453, Jacques de Sauvage, counselor to the king and treasurer of Guyenne, acquired the "tenure rights" to Yquem, which was run by his descendants until 1711. At that time, Léon de Sauvage bought the enfranchisement of the annuity paid to the king, "in return for which the commissioners declare that he will in the future own and maintain these assets in a noble fashion."

On June 6, 1785, Louis-Amédée de Lur-Saluces (whose family name goes back to the sixteenth-century marriage of Jean de Lur with the heir of the marquisate of Saluces) married Françoise-Joséphine de Sauvage, who brought him Yquem as her dowry. He already owned several other estates (Fargues, Malle, Suau). Three years after his marriage he died following a fall from his horse, leaving his widow to face the French Revolution on her own.

In the nineteenth century, the family's possessions grew with the marriage of Françoise-Joséphine's son to Marie-Geneviève de Filhot, whose dowry included the Châteaux Coutet and Filhot.

Their child, Romain-Bertrand, was nicknamed "king of the white vines." The estate then passed into the hands of Amédée de Lur-Saluces, then to his nephew Bertrand. When he died in 1968, the estate was managed by one of his nephews, Alexandre, who shared the property with his older brother Eugène and several other family members.

Alexandre de Lur-Saluces, a tireless promoter of the quality and the international renown of the vineyard, has been fighting to hold on to the estate since 1996, when the world's largest luxury goods group, LVMH (owners of Moët-Hennessy, Louis Vuitton, Dior, etc.) declared that it had taken control of the majority of the capital, bringing the value of Yquem to one billion francs. Alexandre denies this, saying that the joint ownership of the estate prevents such an acquisition. It is now up to the courts to make a decision. In the meantime, the LVMH group, anxious to own such a famous vineyard, has made it known that as owner it would change none of the methods that have made Yquem so famous.

The property has a total area of 420 acres, and the vines take up 247 acres, planted with sémillon (eighty percent) and sauvignon (twenty percent). At best, this could produce 70,000 bottles per year, as yields are very small—only 75 gallons per acre (2,47 acres).

Everything is uncommon in this place that has been admired by generations of wine lovers. Since 1975, Yquem has benefited from a dispensation that allows it to print the obligatory information on a separate band rather than the label itself. All that appears on the austere label is "Château d'Yquem" and "Lur-Saluces," along with the date of the vintage and the crown of a marquis.

Quality control is so strict that sometimes no vintage wine is made from the harvest, as in 1910, 1915, 1930, 1951, 1952, 1964, 1972, 1974, and 1992. When this happens, collectors fill the gap on their shelves with an empty bottle.

Claude Henri Hercule de Lur, marquis de Saluces, and Marie Adelaïde de Maulde, marquise de Lur-Saluces.

The Yquem wine sheds are progressive, yet respectful of tradition. Everything used in the vinification of the wine is made of wood, so as not to affect clarity. If any metal comes into contact with the wine, even a tiny nail in the press, it is enameled to protect the wine. After three months of fermentation, the first racking takes place, and then the wine is aged in barrels for at least three years, with two finings during the first and second year. It is filtered before being bottled.

When young, the wine is a beautiful clear amber; with aging, it takes on the lovely color of burnished gold. Sweet and unctuous, it acquires over the years an unequaled bouquet, finesse, and brilliance. Even after being aged for several decades, it is still astonishingly fresh.

The château, overlooking the entire vineyard, forms a square and has several towers, the oldest of them dating to the fifteenth century. The building itself dates to the seventeenth century and manages to combine rural rusticity with aristocratic majesty.

Sauternes

A deed dated October 15, 1666, made out to François de Sauvage, the tenant of Yquem, stipulates: "To uphold the reputation of the wine, he must not harvest the grapes until they are fully ripe; it is currently the custom in Bommes and Sauternes to undertake the annual harvest around October 15," that is, a month after the usual harvest date in the Bordeaux region. This shows that at least three hundred years ago, and perhaps earlier, it was known that the Sauternes grapes should be picked when they are overripe.

IDENTIFICATION

Type: white wine.

Grape varieties: sémillon (73 percent), sauvignon (21 percent), muscadelle (6 percent).

Area: 1,440 acres (1994).

Production: 792,000 gallons on average.

Characteristics: These golden wines are unctuous but have great finesse. Their highly aromatic bouquet develops after a long period of aging, which can extend to several decades.

The high concentration of Sauternes makes them capable of extremely long aging.

This does not mean that this practice was not known earlier. In fact, in antiquity, the wines called sapriens (*sapros* means "rotten") were known throughout the Mediterranean basin. More recent examples are the *vin de paille* from the French Jura and the *liquoreux* wines of the Loire Valley, but their production is more sporadic and limited in quantity.

A special alchemy takes place in Sauternes because of three factors: the unusual climatic conditions in this area of the Garonne, the over-ripeness of the grapes when they are harvested, and the effects of noble rot, which attacks the interior of the grape and then penetrates the skin. The grape becomes desiccated and wrinkled and crystallizes under the sun. The small amount of juice that is left inside is highly concentrated and contains natural sugars as well as acids and glycerol. This is what makes Sauternes different from, and superior to, other appellations.

The diversity of the soil, which might consist of gravel or clay-limestone, explains the differences between the various Sauternes vineyards. The best wines come from gravelly hilltops. Because of the long-standing fame of the wines, each plot of land in the five towns (Sauternes, Bommes, Fargues, Preignac, and Barsac) that make up the appellation has been carefully studied for many years.

Because the development of noble rot—which is activated by *botrytis*—is so unpredictable, pickers must return to the

same vine several times, picking only those grapes that are ready. This technique, used only for *liquoreux* wines, is referred to as a *trie* in French. (The masculine form, *tri*, refers to the selection of the wine in the cellar). But the number of *tries* has nothing to do with the quality of the wine. Everything depends on the weather conditions and, while it is sometimes necessary to harvest as many as eleven times, some of the very best vintages have required only two *tries*.

History has not recorded the names of those who were the first to let noble rot develop on the Sauternes grapes. This is an entirely natural process that owes nothing to the actions of man, and everything to his inaction: his ability to patiently wait for the ideal moment before picking the grapes.

Many stories and anecdotes have been

told about the birth of the wines of Sauternes. The best known and the most often recounted in the châteaux of the appellation concerns an estate owner who had to go away on a trip and left instructions with his farmer not to pick the grapes until his return. He ended up staying away far beyond the usual date of the harvest, and the grapes had begun to rot. They gave off a great cloud of dust when they were pressed. The juice that they yielded was a wonderful syrup. The hero of the story is said to be the Marquis Romain-Bertrand de Lur-Saluces, the lord of Yquem, who traveled to Russia in 1847. But it just so happens that this was the year of a particularly famous vintage, making the story implausible. A more prosaic explanation involves the wood-pigeon hunt, which takes place at about the same time as the harvest. While wait-

WINE LABELS

Château Doisy was listed in the classification of 1855 as one vineyard, but a complicated inheritance broke up the estate into three separate vineyards, named Doisy-Dubroca, Doisy-Védrines and Doisy-Daëne. It is not always easy for the consumer to understand the Bordeaux appellations, and the matter is further complicated when estates are broken up and the resulting vineyards have such similar names.

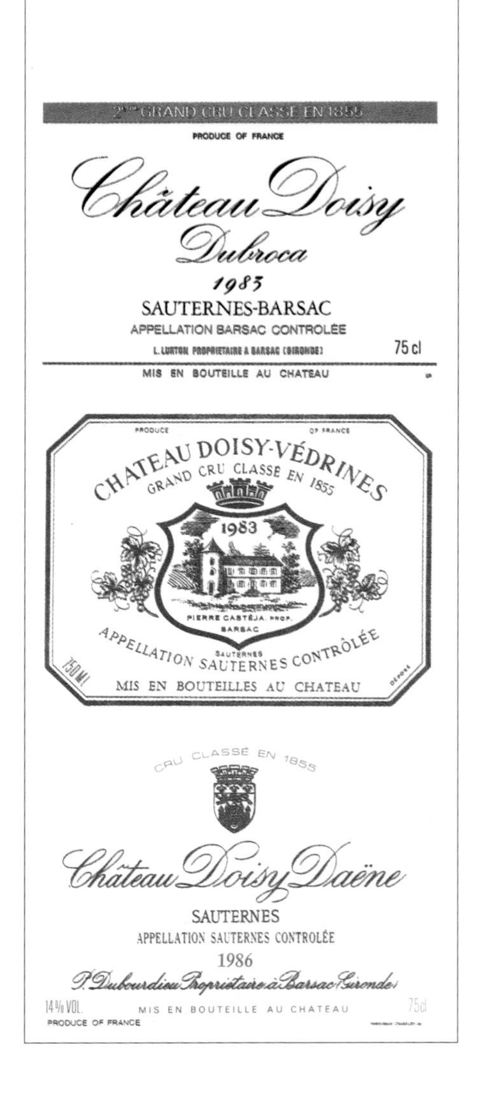

ing in the hides for these highly appreciated migratory birds to pass by, the locals are said to have forgotten to pick the grapes, and that is how they discovered that when the grapes were left on the vine longer they produced a far superior wine.

Whatever the truth of the wine's origins, the mastery of the Sauternes production process came relatively late, around the end of the eighteenth century. Careful surveillance of the vine is required to ensure that it is not affected by gray rot, which would destroy the crop. It is hard to imagine winegrowers taking the risk of losing their crops if they were unaware of the quality that might result.

The yields from these grapes are very small, less than 267 gallons per acre, and only 75 gallons at Yquem, or about one glass of wine per vine. The must contains as much as 400 grams of sugar per liter. The fermentation stops naturally when the alcohol level reaches thirteen or fourteen degrees Celsius. A natural antibiotic called botryticine stops the action of the yeast, leaving a fairly large amount of natural sugar. Then the wine is matured in oak casks, followed by aging, which can last ten years or more. Even after thirty years or more, the *grands crus* have an incomparable freshness, along with unusually complex aromas.

The draconian growing conditions required for Sauternes explain the great variations in the quantities of wines made. In addition, the best vineyards prefer to eliminate or declassify vintages of mediocre quality.

Quite frequently, estates vinify part of their harvest as dry white wines. Even though they are only allowed to use the simple Bordeaux appellation, these are often wines of great quality, especially when they come from the best vineyards, such as Yquem or Rieussec.

Barsac

Located side-by-side, the vineyards of the Barsac and Sauternes appellations are very similar, although Barsac's landscape is slightly less hilly and has more walled estates. The soil and grape varieties are so alike that the two appellations might easily have been rolled into one if it were not for the fact that local variations are taken very seriously in the Bordeaux region.

The Barsac vineyards are allowed to use the Sauternes appellation, but the oppo-

site is impossible, which would seem to indicate that Barsac is just an enclave within a larger appellation. This status was reinforced by the classification of 1855, which listed the best vineyards of the area in the same category.

Some experts think that the wines of Barsac are slightly more *liquoreux* than those of Sauternes, while others find them fresher and more lively. These differences stem from the estates' individual production techniques and soil, which brings out the unique flavors of the best wines.

IDENTIFICATION

Type: white wine.

Grape varieties: Sémillon (73 percent), sauvignon (21 percent), muscadelle (6 percent).

Area: 1,509 acres (1994).

Production: 343,200 gallons on average.

Characteristics: These are unctuous, golden wines that are slightly more *liquoreux* than the Sauternes, to which they are otherwise quite similar.

THE CLASSIFICATION OF SAUTERNES AND BARSAC WINES

The vineyards of Sauternes-Barsac, along with those of the Médoc and Haut-Brion in Graves, were the only ones included in the classification of 1855, proof of the renown the area already enjoyed in the nineteenth century. The hierarchy has not changed since, and Château d'Yquem, rated as a *premier cru supérieur,* holds an exceptional place in the classification (see pages 130-131).

PREMIERS CRUS CLASSÉS

La Tour Blanche. This eighty-four-acre vineyard was not named after the tower depicted on its label, but for Jean de Latourblanche, Louis XVI's treasurer. Its owner at the beginning of the nineteenth century, Mr. Focke, is known for having brought back in 1836 the picking of the grapes by successive *tries,* a practice that had been abandoned at the time because of its cost. In 1909, the estate was bequeathed to the French state by its owner, Daniel Osiris Iffla. He was fascinated by scientific research and wanted the estate to become a viticultural and vinicultural school. Today, the institute enrolls 120 students per year.

Lafaurie-Peyraguet. Formerly the property of the lords of Bommes, the Peyraguey estate owes much of its fame to Mr. Lafaurie, who acquired it during the French Revolution. When it was divided in 1879, the larger part of the estate was renamed Lafaurie-Peyraguey. It became the property of Domaines Cordier in 1917.

Rayne Vigneau. Documents dating as far back as the seventeenth century show that vines have been grown on this estate for centuries. It belonged for a time to the Sauvage family (related to the lords of Yquem), and in the nineteenth century, one of its owners, Catherine de Rayne, made it so profitable that her heirs later added her name to the estate. In 1961, the building and the vineyard were sold separately. After a difficult period, the vineyard, which now belongs to the Mestrezat trading company, is once again producing quality wines.

Suduiraut. The château, built around 1670 and never changed since, is one of the handsomest in the Bordeaux region. The estate is named for an old Gironde family, but the notation *ancien cru du Roy* (former vineyard of the king) on the label is the result of confusion over the name of one of its first owners, Baron Duroy. Quality has often been inconsistent in the past, but the vineyard can produce Sauternes with magnificent finesse and bouquet.

Coutet. From 1788 to 1922, this ninety-five-acre Barsac estate belonged to the Lur-Saluces family, owners of Yquem. It was then purchased by a winepress manufacturer from Lyon, and since 1977, has belonged to an Alsatian industrialist. Throughout, the estate's high level of quality has remained unchanged. Coutet makes a *cuvée speciale,* called Cuvée Madame, using the richest noble-rotted wine, with musts that are naturally from twenty-two to twenty-six degrees. Fruity, and unctuous, Coutet's aromas last longer than almost any other wine.

Climens. Known since the beginning of the sixteenth century, this Barsac vineyard has sixty-two acres planted almost exclusively with sémillon. It belonged to the Roborel family for some time and was then sold after the French Revolution. Problems resulting from joint ownership and the difficulty of finding a buyer after World War II tarnished its former high reputation, and the vineyard was more or less forgotten. It was rescued by Lucien Lurton, who bought it in 1971 and revitalized it. The wine's great finesse and incomparable aromas of orange and honey have led some to consider it equal to Yquem, although in a rather different register.

Clos Haut-Peyraguey. This thirty-seven-acre vineyard was detached from the former Peyraguey estate in 1879 because of an inheritance. The other part is now Lafaurie-Peyraguey, and, in spite of the division, both vineyards are still part of the classification of 1855.

Guiraud. This large estate of 210 acres was listed in the classification of 1855 under the name Bayle and was later renamed for one of its owners. After World War II, it dropped out of sight until 1981, when it was bought by the Narbys, a family of English shipowners. After years of intensive work, they have restored it to its former glory.

Rieussec. Owned by the Carmelite order of Langon before the French Revolution, the vineyard was probably named after the often-dry stream that separates it from Yquem (in French, *ruisseau* means "stream," and *sec* is "dry"). The quality of the wines produced here has always been high, and in 1985, Rieussec became the property of Domaines Barons de Rothschild (Château Lafite-Rothschild), which further refined its powerful style.

RABAUD-PROMIS. The Rabaud estate was run by a single tenant for a long period of time before being divided in two in 1903. The two parts of the estate both retained their ranking in the classification of 1855. Adrien Promis added his name to that of the vineyard when he took it over. He expanded it by annexing Château Peixoto, a *second cru*. The house, designed by Victor Louis (architect of Bordeaux's theater), has a lovely view of Sauternes.

SIGALAS-RABAUD. Named after the owner of the Rabaud vineyard, Henri Drouilhet de Sigalas, it was created from the division of 1903. The vineyard, which once belonged to the Ginestets, has land similar to that of Climens. Since 1949, it has belonged to the Sigalas heirs.

THE OTHER CELEBRITIES

The classification of 1855, which has been modified only once since it was created, does not take into account vineyards that have made their mark in the meantime. Among them are Châteaux Barrejats, Bastor-Lamontagne, Fargues, Claverie, Gilette (a small vineyard that sells only vintages that are at least twenty years old, which are in high demand), Haut-Claverie, Les Justices (whose owner is nicknamed "the antique dealer of Sauternes" because of his collection of old vintages), Raymond-Lafon (which belongs to the family of the former Yquem estate manager and follows the same rigorous methods), and Saint-Amand.

SECONDS CRUS CLASSÉS

- Myrat
- Doisy-Daëne
- Doisy-Dubroca
- Doisy-Védrines
- Arche
- Filhot
- Broustet
- Nairac
- Caillou
- Suau
- Malle
- Romer
- Romer du Hayot
- Lamothe (Despujols)
- Lamothe (Guignard)

Château de Malle, a classified historic monument, is one of the most beautiful châteaux in the Sauternes district. Built by Jacques de Mall in the seventeenth century, the estate has never changed hands and now belongs to Countess Pierre de Bournazel.

Loupiac

The Loupiac appellation was created in 1936 (after that of Cadillac) and concerns only the village of the same name. Its vineyards are very old, but, like the other right-bank appellations, its wines were long considered inferior. Loupiac actually deserves more credit. Its growers take great pains with their wines; they even harvest the grapes in successive *tries*, sometimes more often than for the generic Sauternes.

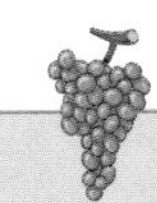

IDENTIFICATION

Type: white wine.

Grape varieties: Sémillon (73 percent), sauvignon (21 percent), muscadelle (6 percent).

Area: 968 acres (1994).

Production: 343,200 gallons on average.

Characteristics: Fruity and lively, these wines have roasted, candied fruit, and honey notes that are especially aromatic.

Although the wines of this appellation do not have the same complexity and richness as those of the left bank, they do, however, possess an interesting aromatic finesse that includes touches of honey. These wines provide good quality for the price because they are still relatively unknown, and a wine lover is better off with a good Loupiac than with an inferior Sauternes.

Despite its small size, the appellation is not entirely homogeneous. The vineyards located near the Garonne River produce more aromatic wines than the inland ones, where it is more difficult for noble rot to produce its effects. The inland wines are more *moelleux* than *liquoreux*. Like all the vineyards on the right bank, the appellation's estate make noble-rotted sweet white wines, but they also produce reds (under the Premières-Côtes appellation) and dry whites. This variety allows the estate owners to compensate for the very high costs of making *liquoreux* wines.

Some of the most prestigious vineyards of the appellation include Château du Cros, which, with 227 acres, is one of the largest in the area; Clos Jean, with its pleasant, elegant wines; La Passonne, with a wide range of aromas in its wines; Loupiac-Gaudiet, whose wines are particularly well balanced; Noble, which is both aromatic and very elegant; Peyrot-Marges, part of the Chassagnol vineyards and producers of many other quality wines, including a rosé; and Terrefort, which makes simple, balanced wines.

Cérons

This small appellation located next to Barsac is surrounded by the Graves vineyards. The wines produced in Cérons can also take the Graves appellation,

something the Barsac producers are not allowed to do. The territory includes the towns of Cérons, Illats, and Podensac. The appellation produces mostly dry white wines and *moelleux* wines (less sweet than the *liquoreux* wines because they have not been transformed by noble rot). Most of the wines are sold under the Graves Supérieur appellation and are better known on foreign markets than in France. A few estates also produce red wines.

Thus, in this area, the production of noble-rotted sweet whites is just one of many activities, unlike in Sauternes, where only *liquoreux* wines are produced. Here, everything depends on climatic conditions, and it often happens that no vintage wines are produced in a given year. Although the *liquoreux* wines of Cérons do not reach the level of quality of those from neighboring appellations, they are known for their finesse and their aromatic bouquet. Two châteaux in particular stand out from the rest: Château de Cérons, owned by the Perromat family, and Grand Enclos du Château de Cérons, which belongs to the Latastes. The Château Huradin, which uses only sémillon grapes for its *liquoreux* wines, is also worth mentioning. The owner of the Château Rahoul in Graves also makes an ample, aromatic Cérons under the name Château La Garance.

IDENTIFICATION

Type: white wine.

Grape varieties: sémillon (73 percent), sauvignon (21 percent), muscadelle (6 percent).

Area: 284 acres (1994).

Production: 66,000 gallons on average.

Characteristics: Similar to those of Sauternes, these wines are characterized by their finesse and vigor and aromas of candied orange peel.

The Cérons estate is a beautiful late seventeenth-, early eighteenth-century charterhouse; it has been producing high-quality cérons for many years.

Sainte-Croix-du-Mont

The winegrowing village of Sainte-Croix-du-Mont has a beautiful view over the Garonne Valley and boasts a special attraction: a bank of fossilized oysters into which caves have been formed. They are now used to display the area's wines.

The appellation has much in common with its neighbor, Loupiac, when it comes to the quality of the wine. The two areas could easily form one appellation were it not for certain local particularities. The soil, grape varieties, and growing and vinification methods are identical, and the two even received their appellation on the same date: September 11, 1936. Some vineyard names, such as Grand Plantier and Peyrot-Marges, are even found in both appellations.

As in Loupiac, there are some bargains to be found in Sainte-Croix-du-Mont, as the wines are increasingly better made and the prices remain reasonable. The return to favor of noble-rotted sweet white wines after a period of unpopularity has not yet caused a surge in prices on the right bank of the Garonne.

The power and finesse of these wines make them a perfect accompaniment to foie gras or Roquefort cheese, and they can also be mixed in cocktails.

Some of the best châteaux are Crabitan-Bellevue, with an elegant, complex bouquet; Grand Plantier, which is currently expanding; La Rame, a good bet for its complexity and refinement; Mont, which has a barrel-aged *cuvée prestige* that reaches the level of a good Sauternes; Loubens, whose owner sometimes waits as long as four years before selling his powerful, well-balanced wine; Pavillon, whose Belgian owners fell in love with the property in the 1980s and produce wines with the aromas of flowers and honey.

IDENTIFICATION

Type: white wine.

Grape varieties: sémillon (73 percent), sauvignon (21 percent), muscadelle (6 percent).

Area: 1,149 acres (1994).

Production: 422,400 gallons on average.

Characteristics: Similar to those of Loupiac, these *liquoreux* wines are lively, with pleasant, fruity notes.

Cadillac

The town of Cadillac, capital of Première-Côtes-de-Bordeaux, has a magnificent, richly decorated château that boasts eight chimneys and was built by the dukes of Épernon. Known as "the Fontainebleau of the Gironde," it now houses a *Maison du Vin.*

The Cadillac appellation was created in 1973 and covers the southern part of Première-Côtes-de-Bordeaux. Noble-rotted sweet white wines are produced here using the same methods applied in Sauternes. Of the three appellations on the right bank of the Garonne that produce liquoreux wines, Cadillac has the smallest production. Most of the Cadillac estates also produce red and dry white wines.

A good part of the production of *liquoreux* whites is sold under the Premières-Côtes-de-Bordeaux appellation, which is more familiar to foreign consumers. Because it includes both *moelleux* and *liquoreux* wines, however, beginners might have some difficulty finding their way around. It is worth deciphering the appelation, however, since the prices are much lower than those of the estates on the left bank of the Garonne.

Wine experts find that the most representative wines of Cadillac come from Clos du Monastère de Broussey, which combines complexity with breeding; Fayau, with its handsome nineteenth-century house, owned by the Medeville family; Jordy d'Orient, whose wine is made exclusively with sémillon grapes and is aged in barrels; Lardiley; Manos; Marsan, now making *liquoreux* wines again after a hiatus of several decades; and Mémoires, which has grown from twelve to ninety-nine acres in ten years and is producing wines of continually increasing quality.

IDENTIFICATION

Type: white wine.

Grape varieties: sémillon (73 percent), sauvignon (21 percent), muscadelle (6 percent).

Area: 2,213 acres (1994).

Production: 79,200 gallons on average.

Characteristics: These wines range from pale yellow to gold, and are fine, light, and somewhat lively, with excellent aromatic qualities. The nose of a good Cadillac can be highly complex, combining apricot and quince with notes of toast and spice cake.

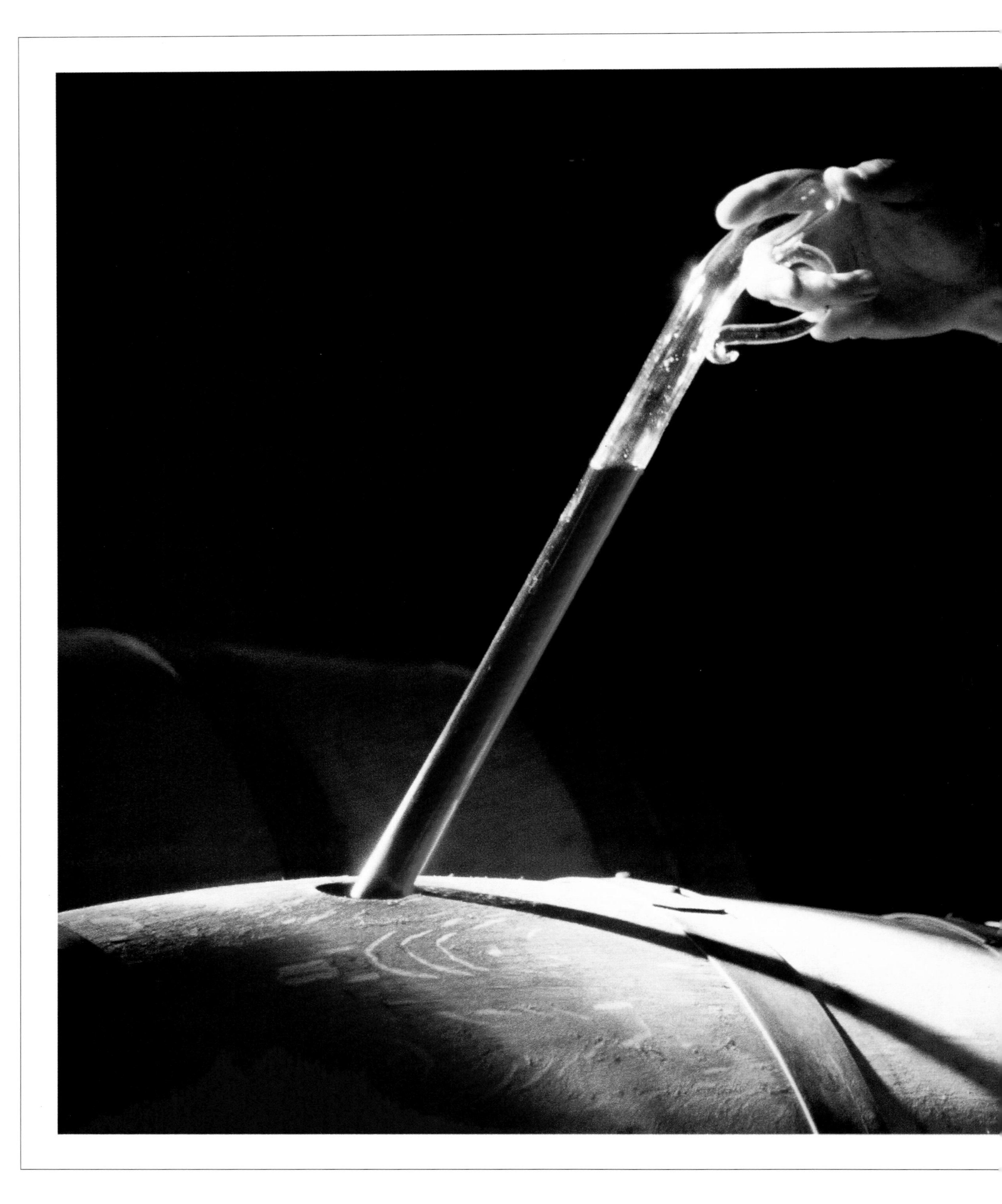

SERVING WINE

The qualities of Bordeaux wines have, and always have had, the power to incite passion and even financial speculation. It must not be forgotten, however, that we are talking about wine, which is, after all, meant to be consumed sooner or later. The major asset of Bordeaux wines is their diversity, and while some of the great *crus* have become inaccessible to ordinary mortals, the Bordeaux vineyards are large enough to supply wines that can satisfy every taste. Both the greatest and the most modest wines deserve consideration when buying, laying down, or serving. Happily, the region's production has reached a generally satisfactory level of quality, and it is rare today to find Bordeaux wines with defects or inadequacies.

Tasting wine can in itself offer a great deal of pleasure, but true satisfaction comes when it is drunk before or during a meal. Be careful not to fall into the trap of label worship, which can lead to the collecting of wines from prestigious châteaux and the loss of the joy of drinking a quality wine. The vineyards of Bordeaux can provide wines that are appropriate to every part of a meal, from the appetizer to dessert, and to every type of food. This search for the perfect match of wine and food is one of the many pleasures offered by the world of wine.

Opposite: The glass pipette *(siphon) used to extract wine from the barrel for tasting* sur fûts, *when the wine has not yet been bottled.*

GRAND VIN
CHATEAU
LYNCH BAGES
GRAND CRU CLASSE
PAUILLAC
APPELLATION PAUILLAC CONTROLEE
1993
13.0% VOL.

THE CARE OF WINE

Once a wine has been purchased, a certain number of precautions must be taken to preserve its quality.

When it is being transported, changes in temperature must be avoided. Transporting a case of fine wine purchased from the producer during a heat wave, for example, is sure to change the wine's nature. In general, wine does not stand up well to shocks, any type of vibrations, and major fluctuations in temperature.

Once a bottle of wine has reached its final destination, it needs to rest for a while to find its balance. It should be kept away from light, if possible in a cool cellar (up to fifteen degrees Celsius, or fifty-nine degrees Fahrenheit) or in a special cabinet designed for the purpose. The most important thing is not so much the temperature itself as a constant temperature. A cellar whose temperature is always over twenty degrees Celsius (sixty-eight Fahrenheit) will cause the wine to age faster.

The bottles should be laid down horizontally so that the wine is in contact with the cork, which prevents it from drying out and letting air into the bottle.

It is a good idea to take red wines out of the cellar a few hours, or even one or two days, before being served. The serving temperature of the wine must still be carefully respected. The practice of serving wine at room temperature dates from the time when cellars and dining rooms were cooler than they are now. Today's heating systems keep the temperature of most homes at 20 degrees Celsius (68 Fahrenheit) or more, which is too warm for most wines.

The serving temperature of a wine is not a secondary consideration; it can have a direct effect on what is perceived during tasting. A fine wine can be ruined if it is served at the wrong temperature. If it is too cold, the tannins will become more aggressive and the acids blurred. If it is too warm, the taste of alcohol is more pronounced and overwhelms the aromas and flavors.

SERVING TEMPERATURES

(Approximate Fahrenheit equivalents in parentheses)

- **From 8 to 10°C** (46.4 to 50°F) for light dry white wines like Entre-deux-Mers, and for rosés and clairets (light reds).
- **From 8 to 10°C** (46.4 to 50°C) for sparkling wines.
- **8°C (46.4°F)** for noble-rotted sweet white wines, with a temperature inversely proportional to the sugar level.
- **From 10 to 12°C (50 to 54°FF)** for unctuous dry white wines like Graves.
- **From 12 to 15°C (54 to 59°F)** for light red wines.
- **From 15 to 18°C (59 to 65°F)** for more tannic, full-bodied red wines and for old vintages. The rule of thumb is to serve the younger red wines at a cooler temperature.

Keep in mind that wine warms up quickly in the bottle and even faster in the glass.

When tasting the same wine from the same year, experts can tell the difference between a bottle that has traveled or been stored in improper conditions from one that is being tasted near the location of its production or, better yet, at the château itself. Pictured below: a tasting at Château Clarke in Listrac, in the Médoc.

The decanting of wine is an often-misunderstood operation. Its main goal is not to eliminate the deposits that are sometimes found at the bottom of a bottle, but to aerate the wine. The deposits are not a defect but the result of a natural phenomenon that is perfectly normal for wines that have been aged for a while. Decanting is appropriate for both red wines and some full-bodied whites.

Decanting airs the wine and allows its aromas to blossom. Opening a bottle a few hours before serving it is not enough to oxygenate the wine because only a tiny part of the surface is in contact with the air.

On the other hand, when wine is poured into a carafe, its bouquet opens up and it reaches its full potential. The act itself is elegant and adds to the pleasure of the experience.

Before it is used, a carafe should first be rinsed and then moistened with a bit of the wine. Young wines should be decanted at least an hour before they are served, and older wines at the last possible moment, as they need less aeration.

Some very old vintages should not be decanted because too much aeration will eliminate the most subtle aromas. It is preferable to serve them in a wine basket, which will help to prevent any deposits from being poured into the glass.

A wine and the dish it is served with should complement and bring out the best in each other. In a perfect alliance between wine and food, new flavors can even be "created" that would not be found in one without the other. But there is no scientific formula for finding the perfect combination, and the best way to discover it is by constant experimentation.

Harmonizing Wine and Food

It is not always easy to choose the right wine to go with a particular dish, but the old taboos and restrictions are no longer so rigidly observed as they once were. Today, is not considered heresy to serve a light red wine with fish, and the combination can even be a great success. The suggestions made below should be considered as possibilities, not obligations.

They are a perfect illustration that there is always a Bordeaux wine that will be appropriate to every occasion.

Aperitif:
A dry white wine, such as Entre-deux-Mers, Côtes-de-Blaye, or Graves; or a cremant or rosé. Among the sweet wines, a Cadillac or a Loupiac is a good choice, but noble-rotted sweet whites should be avoided because they coat the mouth.

Shellfish:
White Bordeaux,
Entre-deux-Mers,
Graves, or a light red.

Cold meats, pâtés:
Bordeaux, Bordeaux Supérieurs,
Côtes-de-Castillon, or Côtes-de-Francs.

Foie gras:
Sainte-Croix-du-Mont, Barsac, Sauternes.

Fried fish:
Entre-deux-Mers, white
or rosé Bordeaux.

Fish with a sauce:
Graves.

White meat and poultry:
White Graves
or a red Côtes wine.

Grilled or roasted meats, leg of lamb:
Médoc, Haut-Médoc, red Graves.

Game birds:
Médoc, Haut-Médoc, red Graves.

Game animals:
Saint-Émilion, Pessac-Léognan,
Fronsac, Pomerol.

One of the great classics of the Gironde is the combination of Sauternes or other **liquoreux** *white wines with Roquefort cheese, an astonishing taste sensation and one of the great gustatory pleasures. The wine's flavors of walnuts, dried fruits, and candied fruits tame the strong taste of the Roquefort, while the Roquefort invigorates the wine.*

Cheese:

It is a good idea to continue with the same wines served with the preceding dish. An exception could be made for Roquefort or other blue cheese, which go very well with *moelleux* or *liquoreux* whites.

Desserts:

Sweet wines are recommended and should be chosen according to the relative sweetness of the dessert being served. Don't be afraid to try a red wine with red fruits (strawberries, raspberries) or a cremant with fruit tarts.

Gastronomy in Bordeaux

The reputation of the cuisine of Bordeaux does not acheive the heights known from that of the Burgundy, Lyon, or Alsace regions, for example. Furthermore, there are far fewer renowned restaurants—not to mention those with Michelin stars—in the area.

This is probably due to the personality of the people of the Gironde, who are not prone to showing off or flaunting their assets. A Bordeaux winegrower, for example, would prefer to invite an important guest to his or her home, while a Burgundian would always take the guest to the best local restaurant.

The great diversity of the wines of the Bordeaux region means that there is one to go with just about any type of cuisine, especially those of high quality. There are not as many regional dishes as wines, however, and they are influenced by the cuisines of Charente and the entire Southwest of France.

Some typical local dishes:

- *Oysters,* green-tinted ones from the Arcachon basin, accompanied by small, slightly spicy grilled sausages or *crépinettes* and served with an Entre-deux-Mers or a Graves.
- *Pibales,* tiny eels that are available only in January and February.
- *Escargots à la Caudéran,* snails simmered in white wine with ham, garlic, and shallots.
- *Cèpes* (meaty wild mushrooms), fried and served with *persillade* (chopped parsley and garlic).
- Lamproie (lamprey eel), a rare, highly prized fish cooked in red wine.
- *Gigot d'agneau de Pauillac,* a leg of lamb with a garlic sauce, delicious with a good Médoc.
- *Agneau cuit en gibelotte,* a lamb fricassee cooked with wine, served with a Sauternes.
- *Cannelés,* little vanilla flavored cakes made with flour and milk and flavored with vanilla that are crispy on the outside and soft inside.

1975
Château
Mouton Rothschild
LE BARON PHILIPPE PROPRIETAIRE
APPELLATION PAUILLAC CONTROLEE
MIS EN BOUTEILLES AU CHATEAU
CHATEAU LAFITE-ROTHSCHILD
1971
APPELLATION PAUILLAC CONTROLEE
MIS EN BOUTEILLE AU CHATEAU
GRAND VIN
DE
PREMIER GRAND CRU CLASSE
1970
GRAND VIN
1978
FRANCE
MIS EN BOUTEILLES
AU CHATEAU

THE BROTHERHOODS OF BORDEAUX

Evocative of the Rabelaisian world of wine, the brotherhoods were created to promote the appellations with which they are associated. Members don costumes of yesteryear, even if they have no direct connection with their ancient predecessors, such as the Enfants-sans-Soucis, which paid dues to the Countess of Gosier-Salé in the sixteenth century; the Ordre de la Méduse and the Ordre de la Boisson de la divine observance (both from the late sixteenth and early seventeenth century); or the Treille, which, during the Fronde, held feasts that were a breeding ground for political opposition.

The modern brotherhoods appeared in France in the 1930s: the Chevaliers du Tastevin of Burgundy was founded in 1934, and the Chevaliers de la Chantpleure of Vouvray in 1937. The associations didn't really become common, however, until after World War II. In lending an aura of medieval folklore to the appellations, winemakers imbued them with the prestige of their ancient roots.

Today, there are more than one hundred wine brotherhoods around the world, with around eighty of them based in France.

The Jurade de Saint-Émilion is one of the best-known Bordeaux brotherhoods. While some people do not approve of the folkloric aspect of the brotherhoods, it is undeniable that they serve a useful public relations role around the world.

The first brotherhood created in the Bordeaux region was the Jurade de Saint-Émilion, founded in 1948. Later, the following groups were organized:

- Commanderie du Bontemps de Médoc et des Graves (1949).
- Connétablie de Guyenne (1952), associated with Côtes-de-Blaye, Entre-deux-Mers, Premières-Côtes-de-Bordeaux, and Graves-de-Vayres.
- Commanderie du bontemps de Sauternes-Barsac (1959).
- Commanderie du bontemps de Sainte-Croix-du-Mont (1963).
- Compagnons du Bordeaux (1966).
- Hospitaliers de Pomerol (1968).
- Gentilshommes du Duché de Fronsac (1969).
- Compagnons du Loupiac (1971).
- Vignerons de Montagne-Saint-Émilion (1981)
- Baillis de Lalande-de-Pomerol (1984).
- Échevins de Lussac-Saint-Émilion and Puisseguin-Saint-Émilion (1987).
- Ordre des chevaliers des vins de Castillon (1994).

The members of these brotherhoods are winegrowers and merchants, and their main goal is to make their appellations better known through the staging of various events, such as the proclamation of the harvest or the Fête de la Fleur, usually accompanied by banquets. They also "enthrone" famous and influential people, thus spreading goodwill and attracting media attention. Among the older brotherhoods, such as the Jurade de Saint-Émilion, these ceremonies have a quasi-official status.

The Commanderies

In 1952, the Grand Conseil du vin de Bordeaux was created, bringing together representatives of the various brotherhoods, delegates of the CIVB, and local government (municipal, departmental, or regional) assemblies. Expanding on the activities of the brotherhoods, their mission is to establish Bordeaux *commanderies* throughout the world. As ambassadors for the wines of the Bordeaux region, these associations, made up of wine lovers and professionals, help to promote the different appellations in their own countries. There are currently fifty-three *commanderies:* twenty-one in the United States, eight in Canada, eighteen in Europe, one in Africa, and five in Asia.

The *commanderies* have a charter and must respect precise rituals. Each one has a "master" who is a respected personality in his or her country and who is not involved in the wine business. While the activities of the commanderies vary, they are always concerned with the promotion of the wines of Bordeaux.

La Fête de la Fleur takes place at the end of June in the Médoc and is celebrated on a different estate each year. The celebration pictured here is at Château d'Issan. The event marks the flowering of the vines and provides an occasion for several brotherhoods to get together in the company of winegrowers and important guests from around the world.

L' Académie du Vin de Bordeaux

Founded in 1947 by a group of well-known merchants and winegrowers, the Académie du Vin de Bordeaux, modeled on the Académie Française, has forty members, including some of the owners of the largest vineyards and notables from the realms of literature, art, science, and academia. Its role is to disseminate the spirit, history, and culture of the wines of Bordeaux in France and abroad by sponsoring publications and events. Its associate members include estate owners, merchants, and wine brokers.

To increase its influence, it also names as honorary members personalities who aid in the promotion of wine.

This beautiful wine cellar is not in a Bordeaux château, but in the heart of Paris. It is the cellar of the Caves Taillevent, on Rue du Faubourg-Saint-Honoré.

BUYING GUIDE

The wine of Bordeaux is naturally associated with the image of a château, even if its name is not always mentioned on the label. The term "château" actually refers to a winegrowing estate that makes its own wines. Usually, the wine is also bottled on the estate as well (although this is not obligatory). In most cases, there is no real château on the estate at all, only the home in which the owners live and the outbuildings where the wine is produced. Sometimes there are no buildings at all.

When the word "château" (or, rarely, "clos" or "domaine") appears on a label, its purpose is to designate either an estate that can be easily located or a wine made by a cooperative in a specific way. When there is no such mention, it can mean several different things:

• The wine is the second wine made from the blending of wines from different vats.

• The wine is a selection (or blend) made by a merchant or a cooperative, which should be clearly indicated on the label. It might come from any vineyard in the Bordeaux region or from a single appellation.

• The wine is a commercial brand, usually owned by a merchant or a cooperative.

A Bordeaux wine label contains some obligatory information and some that is optional.

The obligatory information includes:

• The *appellation d'origine contrôlée* (AOC), which concerns nearly all of the production of Bordeaux, as only a tiny amount (less than two percent) of the region's total production is made up of table wines, most of which are blends that make no mention of the origin of the wine. The AOC corresponds to a description of the area, the region, or the locality where the wine originated. It defines strict conditions of production: a limited geographic area, grape varieties, yields, alcohol content, and winegrowing and winemaking techniques. Production conditions are defined by a *décret de contrôle,* and the wines must be submitted to a preliminary tasting for approval to have the right to use the appellation.

• The alcohol content (in percentage of volume).

• The identification number of the lot, which may also be mentioned on the seal or on the label on the back of the bottle.

Among the optional descriptions on the label, the producer can mention the following:

• *Grand Vin,* as long as it is followed by the name of the appellation. This description has no official status and is not a guarantee of quality.

• A graphic representation of the château, the estate, or the brand name.

• The year, which indicates that the wine is made exclusively from one year's harvest.

• The name of the estate, the vineyard, the château, or the brand name, possibly accompanied by the address.

• The volume of wine contained in the bottle.

When the label says that the wine was *mise en bouteille au château* or *mise en bouteille à la propriété* it means that it was bottled on the estate itself. When it says *mise en bouteille dans la région de production,* it means that it may have been bottled anywhere within the Bordeaux region, most likely by a wine merchant. If the bottling site is not mentioned at all, it usually, but not necessarily, means that it was done outside of the Gironde and that the wine was purchased in bulk.

Where to Buy Wine

The wines of the Bordeaux region were long sold mostly by trading companies, which handled the bottling, packaging, and distribution. This is no longer the case, especially on the French market. The producers themselves are increasingly selling directly to the market after having made and bottled the wines themselves.

This does not mean that you can buy wine from

A collection of old vintages at Château Camensac in the Médoc. Sought-after bottles like these won't be found in the traditional retail circuits, but at wine auctions or on the estate of the producer.

any estate and be sure of getting a good deal, especially when it comes to the most highly rated wines. Prices depend on the fame of the vineyard, the value of the vintage, and on the general demand, especially in export markets.

Right: Racking at Pétrus.

Below: Four bottle sizes of Médoc crus classés: impériale, magnum, double magnum and jéroboam. Except for the magnum (1.5 liters or 1.6 U.S. quarts), which is relatively common, these larger containers are rarely used. In general, wine ages more slowly in them than in standard bottles.

In reality, unless a consumer buys directly from the producer, he or she has no way of knowing whether the wine was shipped directly from the château to the seller or first passed though the hands of a series of middlemen.

According to the CIVB, very little wine is actually purchased in the region of production, representing only six percent of total sales on the French market in 1994. Most is sold through mass distribution (in hypermarkets and supermarkets), which accounts for three-quarters of the wine sold to individuals in France.

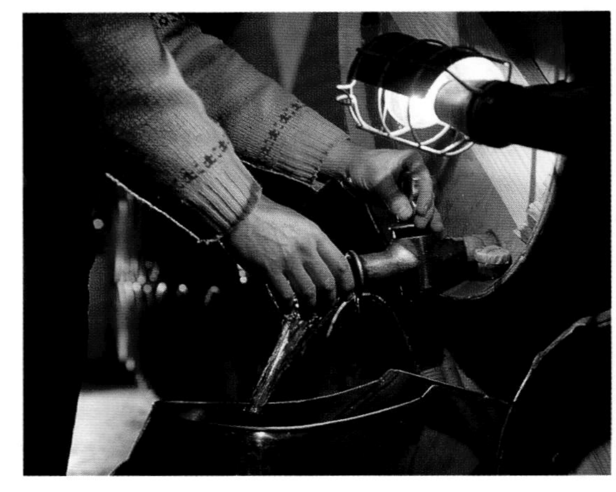

For several years now, the *CIVB* has been organizing wine fairs in September and October at which large amounts of Bordeaux wines are sold. Many bargains can be found at these fairs, and buyers for supermarkets obtain substantial price reductions by buying large lots from producers or merchants. Prudence is recommended, however. Not all prices are discounted, and you should know the vineyards and appellations to avoid making errors.

The main problem with shopping for wine in supermarkets is that the consumer is left alone with the selection of wines on the shelves. Rarely are there knowledgeable salespeople on hand to give advice on the choice of wine and to explain the characteristics of the wines, when they should be drunk, and so on.

This is why specialized outlets, such as cellar owners or mail-order wine companies, still play an indispensable role in advising consumers on which wines to buy. This is especially true for Bordeaux wines as there is such a large number of châteaux and producers in the region. In addition, these professionals are aware of excellent vineyards that are not well known, and they have helped to resurrect some forgotten appellations, especially among the Bordeaux côtes.

Those who are looking to improve their knowledge of Bordeaux wines would do well to join a club or a wine-tasting group. There are many of these in France now, and the cost is usually modest. Members learn about tasting techniques and the characteristics of different appellations and vintages.

Buying wines en primeur: *A Bordeaux Specialty*

Most Bordeaux wines, and especially those of the best appellations, need to be barrel-aged for a year or two before being bottled. For several years now, producers and merchants have been selling wine as soon as it is put in the barrels, that is, only a few months after the harvest, usually in March or April.

The buyer pays a predetermined price, usually less than what would be charged for bottled wine, and receives the wine a year or two later, when the producer decides that its aging is finished. The buyer gets a good deal, and the producer gets the cash ahead of time.

This system of selling *en primeur* has become widespread in Bordeaux, the only winegrowing region that practices it on such a large scale. It provides essential indicators of wine prices and the volumes bought and sold.

For the buyer, however, the risks are such that it is almost like playing the lottery. Only a great connoisseur is really capable of judging the quality of a vintage when the wine is so young, only a few weeks old. Anyone who is thinking of buying at this stage should seek expert advice first, although there are no real objective criteria, such as diplomas or tests, by which to judge an expert's competence. There are only reputations that may or may not be justified. And these experts, some of them self-proclaimed, often have a tendency to announce a bit too quickly that a vintage is the best of the century.

Great caution is therefore advisable when purchasing *en primeur* wines if the buyer is not a specialist who takes the time to visit many wine sheds and taste many wines before making a choice. At the very least, the buyer should compare the critiques available and gather as much information as possible, always remaining wary of the many promises of "great wines from a great vintage year at low prices."

The prices charged for wines *en primeur* are not always based on the quality of the wine—more likely they are based on the rules of supply and demand. Because such large quantities of Bordeaux wines are exported, their prices depend heavily on sales to the United States and the Far East. An example is the phenomenon of the "French paradox," which has increased the popularity of French wines since the middle of the 1990's, when several medical studies revealed that the moderate consumption of red wine helps to diminish the risks of cardiovascular disease and slow the effects of degenerative disease likes Alzheimer's. As a result, sales of red Bordeaux wines have risen, along with their prices. At the same time, interest in wine among Asians has also grown (to the detriment of sales of Cognac).

Preparation for the insertion of the bungs in two-year-old-wine barrels. This bung is make of cork, and a piece of cheesecloth will be inserted between it and the opening in the barrel.

Opposite page: A rare bottle of Lafitte (now Château Lafite-Rothschild), which was sold at Christie's in June 1988. Before the sale, its original cork was changed by the château's **maître de chai** *(cellar master). The most prestigious châteaux provide the service of changing old, damaged corks, and, if the vintage is not too old, the bottle is topped up before inserting the new cork.*

BUYING TIPS

The wine lover who wishes to buy Bordeaux wines, especially *en primeur,* should keep the following principles in mind:

- There is absolutely no uniformity in the quality of a vintage throughout the entire Bordeaux region. Even in the best years, the wines of some appellations might be disappointing and those of some vineyards more mediocre than others.
- The prices of wines sold *en primeur* are not necessarily lower than those of bottled wine. Fluctuations in world prices during the waiting period might cause prices, to fall sometimes by a substantial amount.
- Nevertheless, buying *en primeur* is, in many cases, the only way to procure wine in volume from vineyards with a limited production. Some winegrowers now sell almost all their wine this way, and their bottled wine rarely shows up on the market, even among specialist suppliers.
- When buying *en primeur,* always go directly to the producer and avoid intermediaries agents, whose reputations and financial means can be dubious. There is always the possibility that they go bankrupt, especially when there are great fluctuations in prices, and receipts for the purchase of wines *en primeur* are not worth much beside with other claims.

A triple magnum sold at auction by Christie's. The label was signed by Andy Warhol on April 12, 1979. Warhol illustrated this label for the 1975 vintage at the request of Baron Philippe de Rothschild.

Wine Auctions

The other place to buy wine is at public auctions, at which Bordeaux wines are in high demand. These take place both at auction houses and during special sales of lots of wine from, for example, a restaurant that is emptying its cellar.

Auctions provide an opportunity to buy the very best wines and the rarest vintages that are not available on other markets. But, once again, caution is advised when it comes to both quality and prices.

Naturally, an interested buyer should be very familiar with the appellations and vineyards, but he or she should also be informed about the history of the bottles on offer. Were they conserved in the proper conditions? Did they change hands several times during their existence? Have they traveled a great deal? If this information is not available, buyer beware.

As for prices, there is no official guide, in spite of the efforts of specialist publications and annual guides to provide such information. The authors of these publications base their estimates on the results of all the public sales in France, about one hundred of which are held per year, and establish an average price for each vineyard and each vintage. Only the vineyards whose wines were actually sold are listed, meaning that many respected vineyards are left out. These guides can be useful but are not definitive.

The amateur must also take into account that it is not the quality of the bottle that counts at these sales, but its rarity. This is a speculative system in which a number of participants are looking to make a profit by buying low and selling high—they are not there to build up a wine cellar for their own pleasure.

At these auctions, presided over by a certified auctioneer, bids are made by raising your hand. Be careful to avoid overbidding in the fever of the moment: the price paid might end up exceeding the real value of the wine. And don't forget that a surcharge of a little more than ten percent is added to the amount of the winning bid.

1811
CHATEAU LAFITTE
BORDEAUX

INDEX

of wines and wine areas

ACKNOWLEDGEMENTS

We would like to thank :

Valérie Vrinat and the staff of the Caves Taillevent for their help in organizing the photographic sessions.

Hervé Guillot from the Caves Royales in Versailles.

The many Bordeaux vintners who generously provided samples and documentations.
Mr Jean Zaluski from the Janyse company for providing the sommelier uniform photographed on the cover.
And Christophe Deleval.

The bottle on the cover comes from the wine cellar of the Contre Allée restaurant.

Les Caves Taillevent
199, rue du Faubourg Saint-Honoré, 75008 Paris
Tel. : 01 45 61 14 09
Fax : 01 45 61 19 68

Aux Caves Royales
6, rue Royale, 78000 Versailles
Tel. : 01 39 50 14 10

Société Janyse
66, rue du Faubourg-Saint-Martin, 75010 Paris
Tel. : 01 42 00 16 68
Fax : 01 42 39 21 52

La Contre Allée
83, avenue Denfert-Rochereau, 75014 Paris
Tel. : 01 43 54 99 86
Fax : 01 43 25 05 28

PHOTO CREDITS

All the photographs are by Philippe Hurlin and Matthieu Prier, with the following exceptions :
p. 4 (Christian Braud/DIAF), p. 6 (Jérôme Prébois), p. 7 (Jérôme Prébois), p. 11 (Michel Guillard/SCOPE),
p. 13 (D.R), p. 14 (bottom, Patrick Somelet/DIAF), pp. 16-17 (D.R), p. 19 (Jean-Daniel Sudres/DIAF),
p. 20 (bottom, Jean-Luc Barde/SCOPE, top, D.R), p. 22 (Jérôme Prébois), p. 27 (Patrick Somelet/DIAF),
pp. 30-31 (Michel Guillard/SCOPE), p. 37 (Jérôme Prébois), p. 40 (Christian Braud/DIAF), p. 41 (Jean-Daniel Sudres/DIAF),
p. 42 (Christian Braud/DIAF), p. 60 (D.R), p. 63 (D.R), p. 72 (Christian Braud / DIAF), p. 75 (D.R), p. 78 (Jacques Sierpinski),
p. 79 M. Mastrojanni/DIAF), p. 91 (Jacques Sierpinski/DIAF), p. 96 (Patrick Somelet/DIAF), p. 97 (Gilles d'Auzac),
p. 98 (bottom, D.R), pp. 102-103 (Jérôme Prébois), p. 108 (bottom, Jean-Daniel Sudres/DIAF),
p. 116 (at right and bottom, Patrick Somelet/DIAF), p. 117 (Patrick Somelet/DIAF), p. 118 (Patrick Somelet/DIAF),
p. 120 (Jean-Luc Barde/Scope), p. 121 (Christian Braud/DIAF), p. 122 (Patrick Somelet/DIAF), p. 127 (D.R),
p. 128 (Christian Braud), p. 129 (D.R), p. 132 (bottom, Christian Braud/DIAF), p. 137 (Patrick Somelet/DIAF),
p. 139 (Jacques Sierpinski/DIAF), p. 142 (Christian Braud/DIAF), p. 143 (Guittot/DIAF),
p. 144 (Jean-Daniel Sudres/DIAF), p. 145 (Jacques Sierpinski/DIAF),
p. 146 (top, Christian Braud/DIAF, bottom R. Rosenthal/CIVB), p. 147 (P. Jouard/CIVB),
p. 148 (center, Jean-Daniel Sudres/DIAF), p. 149 (Guittot/DIAF), p. 150 (Patrick Somelet/DIAF),
p. 151 (Christian Braud/DIAF), p. 153 (Jacques Sierpinski/DIAF), p. 154 (top, Jean-Daniel Sudres, bottom, D.R),
p. 155 (Patrick Somelet/DIAF), pp. 156-157 (D.R)